# ALL NEW American LOGO

# ALL NEW American Logo

Madison Square Press

FATHOMS

*design firm* David Carter Graphic Design
*designer* Tien Pham
*art director* Lori Wilson
*client* Atlantis Resort and Casino
*logo for* Fathoms/Nassau, The Bahamas.

MANUFACTURING COUNTS
CHICAGO | 1999 YEAR OF THE SMALL MANUFACTURER

*design firm* ComCorp, Inc.
*designer* Ron Alikpala
*art director* Abby Mines
*client* Chicago Manufacturing Center
*logo for* 1999 Year of the Small Manufacturer Conference (web, print, video).



As this book is printed in four-color process, a few of the designs reproduced here may appear to be slightly different than in their original reproduction.

CB ISBN 0-942604-77-6, PB ISBN 0-942604-78-4
Library of Congress Catalog Card Number 00 130503
Cover art by Frank Lacano

Book and cover designed by Dutton & Sherman

Published by:
Madison Square Press
10 East 23rd Street
New York, NY 10010

Fax (212) 979-2207
e-mail MadisonSqPress@AOL.com

Distributed in North American to the trade and art markets by North Light Books, an imprint of F/W Publications, Inc.
1507 Dana Avenue, Cincinnati, Ohio 45207
*1-800/289-0963

Distributed throughout the rest of the world by:
Hearst Books International, an imprint of HarperCollins
10 East 53rd Street, New York, NY 10019

Printed in Hong Kong

Acknowledgments:
This book wouldn't have been possible without the help and dedication of Arpi Ermoyan or the creative talents of Dutton & Sherman. A big thanks to all the graphic designers who made these great logos available for publication.

# Contents


*Introduction* 6

*Designs based on animals* 10

*Designs based on architecture* 18

*Designs based on arcs* 30

*Designs based on birds* 36

*Designs based on energy bolts* 40

*Designs based on eyes* 42

*Designs based on faces* 44

*Designs based on film, video, and photography* 52

*Designs based on food* 56

*Designs based on globes* 66

*Designs based on hand-drawn letterforms* 70

*Designs based on hands* 80

*Designs based on human figures* 84

*Designs based on initials* 98

*Designs based on internet technology* 120

*Designs based on music* 132

*Designs based on mythology* 138

*Designs based on nature* 140

*Designs based on numbers* 146

*Designs based on objects* 148

*Designs based on ornaments* 156

*Designs based on picturesque views* 160

*Designs based on sea life* 168

*Designs based on shapes* 172

*Designs based on signets* 180

*Designs based on spirals* 190

*Designs based on sports* 192

*Designs based on stars* 200

*Designs based on travel* 202

*Designs based on typography* 208

*Designs based on water* 222


| | |
|---|---|
| *design firm* | Kevin Akers Designs |
| *designer* | Kevin Akers |
| *client* | Motorcycle Industry Council |
| *logo for* | Promotion of motorcycle sports. |

DISCOVER TODAY'S MOTORCYCLING

# Introduction

In early times when few people could read or write, merchants hung pictures over the doors of their establishments to convey their ideas and depict what they sold. In America, a country of immigrants, many were literate but only in a language other than English. As more and more goods and services became available, it became increasingly important to distinguish one tradesman from another. It was but a short step to using symbols to identify which tradesmen made which product or offered which service. The symbols were easily identified and sometimes carried a message for those who could read.

These then were the first brandmarks and the first logos. Today many of those items are much sought after as antiques or wall decorations. While those symbols were a necessity for thousands of years, today we have more sophisticated ways of passing on this kind of information.

RUNNING IRON RESTAURANT AND SALOON

*design firm* The Wecker Group
*designer* Robert Wecker
*illustrator* Mark Savee
*client* Running Iron Restaurant
*logo for* Signage, T-shirts.

| | |
|---|---|
| *design firm* | The Flowers Group |
| *designer* | Cory Shehan |
| *illustrator* | Tracy Sabin |
| *client* | The Ridge |
| *logo for* | Rustic golf resort. |

The earliest marks were very straightforward, but as more competition developed the mark expanded to include humor, puns, satire and even a bit of whimsy. Fred Cooper's symbol for New York Edison Company was dropped after many decades of use in the name of progress, but Mr. Peanut is still with us and still looking through his monocle. Both were used to identify a product and both used a light touch.

Isaac Newton said "For every action there is reaction." It is also true that each period of art is a reaction to the period that preceded it. Graphic design is no exception. The styles favored in the late 1800s and early 1900s were more personal statements. The fine work done in France and England during the Edwardian era, along with the Viennese Secessionist movements, were all hands-on movements. With the Word War I Armistice came Art Deco, a style that captures the imagination with a cross between the mechanical shapes of the draftsman and the artist's irrepressible spirits.

| | |
|---|---|
| *design firm* | Mortensen Design |
| *designer* | PJ Nidecker |
| *art director* | Gordon Mortensen |
| *client* | Handspring, Inc. |
| *logo for* | High-tech company. |

*design firm* MJR Associates
*designer* Aimee McKirdy
*art director* Frank Ruiz
*client* California Sprouts
*logo for* Corporate identity used on stationery, signage and marketing materials.

As the great depression was ending, some remarkable marks begin to appear. They were strong, clever, highly imaginative and subjective. They have stood the test of time very well and one would be hard pressed today to tell a mark created in 1936 from one right out of today's computer. Since that time the trademark has grown increasingly refined and distilled.

As the larger companies expanded into new and more diversified markets the graphics they chose became less related to the companies' beginnings and were in some cases abstract. The most used logos of the time were difficult to identify—they were abstractions that reveal nothing about the identity of the company they represented. As we have passed into the new millennium this fact is still true and in some cases the largest companies have expanded and diversified to the extent that no one any longer remembers what their original product was. One has only to ponder the Time/Warner merger with AOL, forming one company that in some sense does everything.

*design firm* The Huge Idea
*designer* Lesli Wuco-B
*client* For Pets' Sake.com
*logo for* Company/Website.

*design firm* Vigon/Ellis
*designers* Marc Yeh, Brian Jackson
*art director* Larry Vigon
*client* Gravity Games
*logo for* Corporate identity.

Within the last decade of the 20th century things began to change. Humor and whimsy and the craft of graphic design began to slip back into the pictures. The "ALL NEW" logo is now, the marks are more quirky; what's new is beginning to look a lot like what's old. The charm and personality of the past has a decidedly "ALL NEW" look and flavor. "ALL NEW AMERICAN" is more eclectic, more colorful and more subjective.

As the new millennium starts it has been said that the new logo is not necessarily a new phenomenon. There have always been those marks, usually created for small, creative companies that relied upon personality, wit and charm. Often the marks were created for designers and agencies for self promotion. But today, led by the music and entertainment industries, and followed closely by the clothing and computer industries, the "ALL NEW AMERICAN" logo is appearing more often. These observations and ideas are now more mainstream; many logos are again making a statement about whom or what they represent, and the change can be seen as some of the world's largest companies convert their marks to show them as they are today.

*design firm* Miriello Grafico, Inc.
*designer* Chris Keeney
*client* Microlink

BEELine
MEDIA SERVICES

*10.1*

BRAEMAR
COUNTRY CLUB

*10.2*

*10.3*

*10.1*
*design firm* The Wecker Group
*designer* Robert Wecker
*client* Bee Line Media Services
*logo for* All applications.

*10.2*
*design firm* Vigon/Ellis
*designer* Marc Yeh
*art director* Larry Vigon
*client* Braemar Country Club
*logo for* Corporate identity.

*10.3*
*design firm* Fitch
*designer* Cris Logan
*art director* Vassoula Vasiliou
*client* Kärna LLC
*logo for* Product brand identity, packaging, merchandising, web for new gamer mouse.

*11.1*
*design firm* Vigon/Ellis
*designer* Brian Jackson
*art director* Larry Vigon
*client* Glen Annie Golf Club
*logo for* Corporate identity.

*11.2*
*design firm* Vigon/Ellis
*designer* Brian Jackson
*art director* Larry Vigon
*client* Virtualis
*logo for* Corporate identity.

*11.3*
*design firm* Blanco Design
*designer* Shelly Blanco
*client* Return to Freedom

*11.4*
*design firm* Leeson Design
*designer* Susan Leeson
*client* Animalia Publishing Company
*logo for* Animal-focused publishing company.

*11.5*
*design firm* Sandy Gin Design
*designer* Sandy Gin
*client* WOMBATS
*logo for* Women's Mountain Bike & Tea Society.

Glen Annie Golf Club

11.1

VIRTUALIS

11.2

Return to Freedom

11.3

Animalia
PUBLISHING COMPANY

11.4

WOM Bats

11.4

12.1

12.2

12.3

12.1
*design firm* Zamboo
*art director* Dave Zambotti
*client* Doggone Gourmet
*logo for* Corporate identity.

*12.2*
*design firm* Michael Osborne Design
*designer* Andy Cambouris
*art director* Michael Osborne
*client* University of the Pacific
*logo for* Department of athletics.

*12.3*
*design firm* Morreal Graphic Design
*designer* Mary Lou Morreal
*client* Upper Deck
*logo for* Trading card.

*13.1*
*design firm* Phillips Ramsey
*art director* Kevin Stout
*illustrator* Tracy Sabin
*client* San Diego Zoo
*logo for* Promotional car sticker for the zoo.

13.2
*design firm* John Champ Design Associates
*designer* Randall Cohen
*client* KCBS/KLLC Radio Alice@97.3
*logo for* Event identity for 5-mile run/walk and concert.

*13.3*
*design firm* Blanco Design
*designer* Shelly Blanco
*client* Lucky Dog Records

*13.4*
*design firm* Klass Design
*designer* Logo Doctor
*art director* Teri Klass
*illustrators* Tim Clark, Teri Klass
*client* Intelynx
*logo for* Identity for an international investment company.

13.1

13.2

13.3

13.4

14.1

14.2

14.3

14.4

14.5

15.1

15.2

15.3

14.1
*design firm* Mike Salisbury Communications
*designer* Logo doctor
*art director* Mike Salisbury
*illustrator* Tim Clark
*client* Red Ant Production
*logo for* Identity proposal for production company.

14.2
*design firm* Carol Gravelle Graphic Design
*designers* Carol Gravelle, Shannon Karen
*client* ABBY Radio Station
*logo for* Station identity.

14.3
*design firm* Lawless Graphic Design
*designer* John P. Lawless
*client* Planet Magic Productions
*logo for* Retail line of magic and games for The Magic Vault.

14.4
*design firm* AKA Studios
*designer* Logo Doctor
*art director* Dave Brzyowski
*illustrator* Teri Klass
*client* Legacy
*logo for* Identity and packaging for fine linen company.

14.5
*design firm* The Stricklin Companies
*designer* Julie Ann Stricklin
*art director* Steve Emtman
*client* Steven Charles Emtman/Defender Films
*logo for* New company identity for title art, marketing, film identity.

15.1
*design firm* Bryan Friel Studio
*designer* Bryan Friel
*client* Rahn's Pecans
*logo for* Packaging, ads, website.

15.2
*design firm* BobCo Design Inc.
*designer* Robert S. Nenninger
*client* The Crazy Horse SteakHouse
*logo for* Identity for a restaurant and concert venue. A country music legend that is moving to more upscale facilities.

15.3
*design firm* Earlywine Design
*designer* Terry Earlywine
*client* Tigera Corporation
*logo for* Corporate identity, packaging, stationery.

*16.1*
*design firm* De Muth Design
*designer* Roger De Muth
*art director* Ned Eisenberg
*illustrator* Roger De Muth
*client* Mama Gorilla
*logo for* Restaurant signage, ads, T-shirts, etc.

*16.2*
*design firm* De Muth Design
*designer* Roger De Muth
*client* De Muth Design
*logo for* All printed materials used by artist.

*16.3*
*design firm* De Muth Design
*designer* Roger De Muth
*art director* Connie Potter
*illustrator* Roger De Muth
*client* Once Again Nut Butter
*logo for* Peanut butter/nutbutter company identity.

*17.1*
*design firm* Alexander Atkins Design, Inc.
*designer* Alexander Atkins
*client* University of California, Berkeley
*logo for* Alumni event.

*17.2*
*design firm* Dutch Design
*designer* Rick Smits
*client* Ambrosi and Associates
*logo for* Proposed logo for fund-raising marathon T-shirt art.

*17.3*
*design firm* Sandy Gin Design
*designer* Sandy Gin
*client* Sandy Gin Design
*logo for* Promotional logo for design studio.

*17.4*
*design firm* De Muth Design
*designer* Roger De Muth
*art directors* Felicia Recht, Naomi De Muth
*illustrator* Roger De Muth
*client* Chameleon Gallery
*logo for* Gallery signage, ads, posters, etc.

*16.1*

*16.2*

*16.3*

17.1

17.2

17.3

17.4

*18.1*
*design firm* Michael Osborne Design
*designer* Michelle Regenbogen
*art director* Michael Osborne
*illustrator* Michelle Regenbogen
*client* Margrit Biever Mondavi
*logo for* Theatre at Opera House.

*18.2*
*design firm* Kevin Akers Designs
*designer* Kevin Akers
*client* Tindell House
*logo for* English bed and breakfast.

*18.3*
*design firm* Carol Gravelle Graphic Design
*designer* Carol Gravelle
*client* Creative Concrete & Design
*logo for* Company identity.

*19.1*
*design firm* Sabingrafik, Inc.
*designer* Tracy Sabin
*art director* Marilee Bankert
*illustrator* Tracy Sabin
*client* Oliver McMillin
*logo for* Shopping/entertainment center.

*19.2*
*design firm* Kevin Akers Designs
*designer* Kevin Akers
*client* Hilton Hotels
*logo for* Advertising icon.

*19.3*
*design firm* Carlson Marketing
*designer* Logo Doctor
*art director* Norm Tribe
*illustrator* Tim Clark
*client* Mazda
*logo for* Promotional brochure and incentive program.

*19.4*
*design firm* Blanco Design
*designer* Shelly Blanco
*client* Times Square Deli

*19.5*
*design firm* Bryan Friel Studio
*designer* Bryan Friel
*client* It's a Grind
*logo for* Signage, ads, packaging.

*19.6*
*design firm* Bruce Yelaska Design
*designer* Bruce Yelaska
*client* Saarman Construction Company
*logo for* 1998 promotional logo for company's advertising campaign.

*18.1*

*18.2*

*18.3*

Gaslamp
SIXTH AVENUE

19.1

One Hilton
One Place to Stay

19.2

MAZDA
TOWN

19.3

Times Square Deli

19.4

IT'S A GRIND
COFFEE HOUSE

19.5

19.6

DUBLIN HOUSE

20.1

NACCA & CAPIZZI
CERTIFIED PUBLIC ACCOUNTANTS LLP

20.2

SALTZ MONGELUZZI
BARRETT & BENDESKY PC
TRIAL LAWYERS

20.3

21.1

21.2

21.3

20.1
*design firm* Allen Orr
*designer* Allen Orr
*client* Dublin House Irish Pub

20.2
*design firm* McElveney & Palozzi Design Group, Inc.
*art director* William McElveney
*client* Nacca & Capizzi LLP
*logo for* Letterhead, business cards, envelopes.

20.3
*design firm* LF Banks + Associates
*designer* John German
*art director* Lori F. Banks
*client* Saltz, Mongeluzzi, Barrett & Bendesky, PC
*logo for* Corporate identity for law firm.

21.1
*design firm* Juddesign
*designers* Eric Watanabe, Rosemary Rae
*art director* Patti Judd
*client* The Campanile Foundation
*logo for* San Diego State University charity organization.

21.2
*design firm* The Wecker Group
*designer* Robert Wecker
*client* San Juan Bautista Chamber of Commerce
*logo for* Stationery, forms.

21.3
*design firm* Kevin Akers Designs
*designer* Kevin Akers
*client* Hilton Hotels
*logo for* CrestHill, a new Hilton hotel property.

22.1

22.2

22.3

22.4

22.1

| | |
|---|---|
| *design firm* | RVH Studio |
| *designer* | Paul Rogers |
| *art director* | Jill Von Hartmann |
| *illustrator* | Paul Rogers |
| *client* | Y3K Productions |
| *logo for* | Chicago-based film production company. |

22.2

| | |
|---|---|
| *design firm* | Heart Times Coffee Cup Equals Lighting |
| *designer* | Paul Rogers |
| *art director* | Bobby Woods |
| *illustrator* | Paul Rogers |
| *client* | HBO |
| *logo for* | New York City production company. |

22.3

| | |
|---|---|
| *design firm* | Dizinno & Partners |
| *art director* | Mike Stivers |
| *illustrator* | Tracy Sabin |
| *client* | Convis |
| *logo for* | Promotion for the San Diego Convention and Visitors Bureau. |

22.4

| | |
|---|---|
| *design firm* | Kevin Akers Designs |
| *designer* | Kevin Akers |
| *client* | San Francisco Symphony |
| *logo for* | Asian tour of San Francisco Symphony. |

23.1

| | |
|---|---|
| *design firm* | John Pound Art |
| *designer* | John Pound |
| *client* | Humboldt Arts Council |
| *logo for* | Promotion and grand re-opening of renovated Carnegie building as an arts museum in Humboldt County, California. |

23.2

| | |
|---|---|
| *design firm* | BobCo Design Inc. |
| *designer* | Robert S. Nenninger |
| *client* | The Golden Gate Bread Co. |
| *logo for* | Product packaging identity for a sourdough bread company that exports to the Japanese market. |

23.3

| | |
|---|---|
| *design firm* | Enigma Design Studio |
| *designer* | Logo Doctor |
| *art director* | Randy Hipky |
| *illustrator* | Tim Clark |
| *client* | Thames |
| *logo for* | Identity for British television station. |

*23.1*

*23.2*

*23.3*

24.1

24.2

24.3

*24.1*

| | |
|---|---|
| *design firm* | The Wecker Group |
| *designer* | Robert Wecker |
| *client* | Robert Rosenthal, Attorney |
| *logo for* | Stationery, forms. |

*24.2*

| | |
|---|---|
| *design firm* | Shields Design |
| *designer* | Charles Shields |
| *client* | Maxim Mortgage Corporation |
| *logo for* | Mortgage company. |

*24.3*

| | |
|---|---|
| *design firm* | Moonlight Design |
| *designer* | David Ryer |
| *client* | Paradigm |
| *logo for* | Investment, financial services company. |

*25.1*

| | |
|---|---|
| *design firm* | Shields Design |
| *designer* | Thomas Kimmelman |
| *art director* | Charles Shields |
| *client* | Paul D. Lerandeau |
| *logo for* | Lawyer. |

*25.2*

| | |
|---|---|
| *design firm* | Calori & Vanden-Eynden |
| *designer* | Chris Calori |
| *client* | Michael Graves & Associates |
| *logo for* | Building designed by Michael Graves & Associates. |

*25.3*

| | |
|---|---|
| *design firm* | Moonlight Design |
| *designer* | David Ryer |
| *client* | Capital Partners |
| *logo for* | Financial services, venture capital firm. |

*25.4*

| | |
|---|---|
| *design firm* | Vinje Design, Inc. |
| *designer* | Andreas Keller |
| *client* | Legacy Partners |
| *logo for* | Symbol for a large commercial and residential real estate company with three major divisions. |

Paul E. Lerandeau
ATTORNEY AT LAW

25.1

ONE
PORT CENTER

25.2

Capital
Partners

25.3

LEGACY
PARTNERS

25.4

26.1
*design firm* Vigon/Ellis
*designer* Daniel Cho
*art director* Larry Vigon
*client* Area 51 Advertising
*logo for* Corporate identity.

26.2
*design firm* Kahnartist Design
*designer* Linda Kahn
*client* Ray Clayton Realty
*logo for* Identity and stationery system.

26.3
*design firm* Taber Integrative Design
*designer* Michele Taber
*client* AP Thomas Construction, Inc.
*logo for* A fast-track, high-tech, multimillion dollar construction company.

27.1
*design firm* Dutch Design
*designer* Rick Smits
*client* Drenth Builders
*logo for* Stationery, business cards and signage.

27.2
*design firm* Allen Orr
*designer* Allen Orr
*client* The Apartment Phone
*logo for* Apartment search.

27.3
*design firm* Eve Vrla Design
*designer* Eve Vrla
*client* Lewis Development Services
*logo for* The Pinnacle in Kierland development project stationery, brochure, signage.

27.4
*design firm* Earlywine Design
*designer* Terry Earlywine
*client* Metropolis
*logo for* Sales automation software company, stationery, signage.

26.1

26.2

26.3

DRENTH
BUILDERS

27.1

27.2

THE
PINNACLE
IN KIERLAND

27.3

METROPOLIS

27.4

28.1

28.2

28.3

28.4

29.1

29.2

29.3

*28.1*

| | |
|---|---|
| *design firm* | Tom Fowler, Inc. |
| *designer* | Karl S. Maruyama |
| *art director* | Thomas G. Fowler |
| *illustrator* | Karl S. Maruyama |
| *client* | Reynolds and Rose |
| *logo for* | A website that dynamically builds a virtual town based on your zip code. |

*28.2*

| | |
|---|---|
| *design firm* | Juddesign |
| *designers* | Heidi Sullivan, Eric Watanabe |
| *art director* | Patti Judd |
| *client* | Home Seekers.com |
| *logo for* | Online real estate resource. |

*28.3*

| | |
|---|---|
| *design firm* | Zamboo |
| *art director* | Cave Zambotti |
| *client* | Dogloo |
| *logo for* | Corporate identity. |

*28.4*

| | |
|---|---|
| *design firm* | GDS Studio |
| *designer* | Gary Solomon |
| *client* | Rent Line |
| *logo for* | Outdoor advertising on bus benches, bus shelters. |

*29.1*

| | |
|---|---|
| *design firm* | Engle + Murphy |
| *designer* | Robin Seaman |
| *client* | The Light House |
| *logo for* | Corporate identity for non-profit organization that provides transitional housing and services for homeless women. |

*29.2*

| | |
|---|---|
| *design firm* | Bruce Yelaska Design |
| *designer* | Bruce Yelaska |
| *client* | Saarman Construction Company |
| *logo for* | 1999 promotional logo for company's advertising campaign. |

*29.3*

| | |
|---|---|
| *design firm* | Conover |
| *designer* | Amy Williams |
| *art director* | David Conover |
| *client* | Addison Homes |
| *logo for* | Custom home builder. |

30.1
*design firm* Bruce Yelaska Design
*designer* Bruce Yelaska
*client* Millennium Restaurant Consultants
*logo for* Restaurant consulting group operating various restaurants in California and outside the United States.

30.2
*design firm* Calori & Vanden-Eynden
*designer* Chris Calori
*client* Arc Properties, Inc.
*logo for* Real estate investment company.

30.3
*design firm* Bruce Yelaska Design
*designer* Bruce Yelaska
*client* The Gauntlett Group
*logo for* Environmental engineering firm. The 2 Gs represent the earth and the company's global greening solutions.

31.1
*design firm* McElveney & Palozzi Design Group, Inc.
*art directors* Steve Palozzi, Jon Westfal
*client* Auto-Soft
*logo for* Sell sheets, software packaging for MCS Two Thousand.

31.2
*design firm* The Wecker Group
*designer* Matt Gnibus
*client* Gnibus Public Relations
*logo for* Stationery.

31.3
*design firm* Foreshock
*designer* Gary Zdeneck
*client* PSP Direct
*logo for* Mortgage broker.

31.4
*design firm* Stewart Monderer Design, Inc.
*designer* Aime Lecusay
*art director* Stewart Monderer
*client* Crescent Networks, Inc.
*logo for* Identity.

30.1

ARC

30.2

30.3

MCS
TWO THOUSAND

31.1

GNIBUS
PUBLIC RELATIONS

31.2

PSP DIRECT
prime / sub-prime

31.3

CRESCENT
networks

31.4

MENLO REALTY

32.1

ORBA

32.2

PRIME COMPANIES, INC.

32.3

creative solutions group

32.4

32.1
*design firm* Wolfback Design
*designer* Karin Scholz
*client* Menlo Realty
*logo for* Realtor.

32.2
*design firm* Zamboo
*art director* Becca Bootes
*client* ORBA Financial Management
*logo for* Corporate identity.

32.3
*design firm* Lamfers & Associates
*designer* Missy Nery
*art director* Debra Lamfers
*client* Prime Companies, Inc.
*logo for* Company identity and applications. PCI invests in and provides management to emerging new technology firms.

32.4
*design firm* Zamboo
*designer* Becca Bootes
*client* Creative Solutions Group
*logo for* Corporate identity.

33.1
*design firm* David Carter Graphic Design
*designer* Tabitha Bogard
*art director* Lori Wilson
*client* Mandalay Bay Resort and Casino
*logo for* Pearl Moon Boutique/Las Vegas, Nevada.

33.2
*design firm* Kevin Akers Designs
*designer* Kevin Akers
*client* Aurea
*logo for* Cordless/wireless headset product.

PEARL MOON
BOUTIQUE

33.1

AUREA

33.2

NICHOLS
CONCRETE CUTTING

34.1

KARAHADIAN

GENERAL DENTISTRY

34.2

DEL VALLE
COMMUNICATIONS

34.3

CALIFORNIA
ACADEMY
OF
SCIENCES

34.4

EFFICIENT
Capital Management, LLC

34.5

35.1

35.2

35.3

| | |
|---|---|
| *34.1* | |
| *design firm* | Earlywine Design |
| *designer* | Terry Earlywine |
| *client* | Nichols Concrete Cutting |
| *logo for* | Company identity, trucks, stationery. |

| | |
|---|---|
| *34.2* | |
| *design firm* | MJR Associates |
| *designer* | Frank Ruiz |
| *client* | Edward & Kari Karahadian, DDS |
| *logo for* | Corporate identity used on stationery, signage and marketing materials. |

| | |
|---|---|
| *34.3* | |
| *design firm* | Alexander Atkins Design |
| *designer* | Alexander Atkins |
| *client* | Del Valle Communications |
| *logo for* | Company specializing in corporate communications. |

| | |
|---|---|
| *34.4* | |
| *design firm* | Primo Angeli Inc. |
| *designer* | Kelson Mau |
| *art director* | Rich Scheve |
| *client* | California Academy of Sciences |
| *logo for* | All uses. |

| | |
|---|---|
| *34.5* | |
| *design firm* | ComCorp, Inc. |
| *designer* | Marnie Breen |
| *art director* | Abby Miesen |
| *client* | Efficient Capital Management |
| *logo for* | Corporate material. |

| | |
|---|---|
| *35.1* | |
| *design firm* | Miriello Grafico, Inc. |
| *designer* | Liz Bernal |
| *client* | Extrovert |

| | |
|---|---|
| *35.2* | |
| *design firm* | Bruce Yelaska Design |
| *designer* | Bruce Yelaska |
| *client* | Simmons, Ungar, Helbush, Steinbert & Bright |
| *logo for* | Immigration law firm. |

| | |
|---|---|
| *35.3* | |
| *design firm* | Stewart Monderer Design, Inc. |
| *designer* | Stewart Monderer |
| *client* | Xyvision Enterprise Solutions, Inc. |
| *logo for* | Identity. |

36.1

36.2

36.3

*36.1*
*design firm* Sandy Gin Design
*designer* Sandy Gin
*client* BlinkingOwl.com
*logo for* An on-line shopping comparison site targeting college students.

*36.2*
*design firm* Tharp Did It
*designers* Rick Tharp, Jana Heer
*client* Bayshore Press
*logo for* An environmentally responsible printer on the West Coast.

*36.3*
*design firm* Juddesign
*designer* Geoff Ledet
*art director* Patti Judd
*client* McMillin Company—Calavera Hills
*logo for* Residential real estate development.

*37.1*
*design firm* MJR Associates
*designer* Frank Ruiz
*client* Riverbend Golf Club
*logo for* Corporate identity used on stationery, signage, vehicles and marketing materials.

*37.2*
*design firm* The Wecker Group
*designer* Robert Wecker
*client* California Insurance Group

*37.3*
*design firm* American Film Institute
*designer* Logo Doctor
*art directors* Tim Clark, Teri Klass
*illustrator* Tim Clark
*client* AFI
*logo for* Identity.

Riverbend
GOLF CLUB

37.1

CALIFORNIA
INSURANCE
GROUP SINCE 1898
TM

37.2

AMERICAN FILM INSTITUTE

37.3

DOUBLE EAGLE

GOLF CENTER

38.1

Cypress Avenue

Baptist Church

38.2

*38.1*
*design firm* Conover
*designer* Melissa Fraser
*art director* David Conover
*client* Double Eagle
*logo for* Golf center.

*38.2*
*design firm* Leeson Design
*designer* Susan Leeson
*client* Cypress Avenue Baptist Church
*logo for* Community Christian church.

*39.1*
*design firm* The Wecker Group
*designer* Robert Wecker
*client* Pelican Pizza
*logo for* Signage, stationery, packaging, forms.

*39.2*
*design firm* Deluxe Brand
*designer* Tor Naerheim
*client* Dimp Wear
*logo for* Line of clothing.

*39.3*
*design firm* Shields Design
*designer* Charles Shields
*illustrator* Doug Hansen
*client* Investment products catalog/store.

PELICAN PIZZA

*39.1*

P

*39.2*

KEN'S TRADING POST

*39.3*

40.1

40.2

40.3

*40.1*
*design firm* GDS Studio
*designer* Gary Solomon
*client* GDS Studio
*logo for* On the Mark, a book compiled of logo designs with background of the development of each mark.

*40.2*
*design firm* Zamboo
*art director* Dave Zambotti
*client* Baton Records
*logo for* Record label corporate identity.

*40.3*
*design firm* Curry Design Associates
*designer* Joy Rubin
*art director* Steve Curry
*lient* Usernet
*logo for* Electronic convention.

*41.1*
*design firm* Kevin Akers Designs
*designer* Kevin Akers
*client* San Francisco Symphony
*logo for* T-shirt graphic for SFS/members of the Grateful Dead concert.

*41.2*
*design firm* Vigon/Ellis
*designer* Brian Jackson
*art director* Larry Vigon
*client* Cyber Media
*logo for* Corporate identity.

San Francisco Symphony
Members of
and
The Grateful Dead

41.1

CYBERMEDIA
MORE POWER TO YOU

41.2

*42.1*

*42.2*

*42.3*

*42.1*

| | |
|---|---|
| *design firm* | Fuse |
| *designer* | Russell Pierce |
| *client* | PairGain (Avidia IQ) |
| *logo for* | Product logo, used on packaging and literature. |

*42.2*

| | |
|---|---|
| *design firm* | LF Banks + Associates |
| *designer* | John German |
| *art director* | Lori F. Banks |
| *client* | The Point |
| *logo for* | Identity image for coffeehouse and concert venue. |

*42.3*

| | |
|---|---|
| *design firm* | Taber Integrative Design |
| *designer* | Barbara Hennelly |
| *art director* | Michele Taber |
| *client* | ChannneLogic |
| *logo for* | An identity for a company that assesses profitability in "Fortune 100" company channel partnerships. |

*43.1*

| | |
|---|---|
| *design firm* | Moonlight Design |
| *designer* | Karen Ryan |
| *client* | Visionsound Productions |
| *logo for* | Audio and video post-production house. |

*43.2*

| | |
|---|---|
| *design firm* | Pierre Rademaker Design |
| *designers* | Pierre Rademaker, Kandy David |
| *client* | Blake Printery |
| *logo for* | Print items, forms, signage, vehicles, uniforms, shipping containers, collateral. |

*43.3*

| | |
|---|---|
| *design firm* | The Wecker Group |
| *designer* | Robert Wecker |
| *client* | Denise Matta |
| *logo for* | Stationery. |

visionsound
PRODUCTIONS

43.1

FINE QUALITY LITHOGRAPHIC PRINTING
SINCE 1949

43.2

DM

DENISE MATTA

PHOTOGRAPHY/ILLUSTRATION/GRAPHIC DESIGN

43.3

44.1

| | |
|---|---|
| *design firm* | John Champ Design Associates |
| *designer* | Randall Cohen |
| *client* | Permagrin |
| *logo for* | Corporate identity. |

44.2

| | |
|---|---|
| *design firm* | Kevin Akers Designs |
| *designer* | Kevin Akers |
| *client* | eQuaint.com |
| *logo for* | Software company. |

44.3

| | |
|---|---|
| *design firm* | Vigon/Ellis |
| *designers* | Marissa Galang, Brian Jackson |
| *art director* | Larry Vigon |
| *client* | Interven Partners |
| *logo for* | Corporate identity. |

45.1

| | |
|---|---|
| *design firm* | VWA Group |
| *designer* | Rhonda Warren |
| *client* | Los Piratas |
| *logo for* | Children's Center for luxury resort. |

45.2

| | |
|---|---|
| *design firm* | Kevin Akers Designs |
| *designer* | Kevin Akers |
| *client* | Bank Street |
| *logo for* | Clothing boutique. |

45.3

| | |
|---|---|
| *design firm* | Kevin Akers Designs |
| *designer* | Kevin Akers |
| *client* | Suissa Beauty Company |
| *logo for* | Beauty products and packaging. |

45.4

| | |
|---|---|
| *design firm* | LF Banks + Associates |
| *designer* | John German |
| *art director* | Lori F. Banks |
| *client* | Center for Greater Philadelphia |
| *logo for* | Identity image for non-profit public policy organization. |

45.5

| | |
|---|---|
| *design firm* | Focus Design |
| *designer* | Brian Jacobson |
| *client* | Black & Co. |
| *logo for* | Corporate identity. |

44.1

44.2

44.3

Los Piratas

45.1

45.2

Center
for Greater Philadelphia

45.3

45.4

Building Brands With Personality

&CO.

45.5

46.1

46.2

46.3

46.1

| | |
|---|---|
| *design firm* | Mortensen Design |
| *designer* | Wendy Chon |
| *art director* | Gordon Mortensen |
| *client* | Tamalpais Bank |
| *logo for* | The bank. |

46.2

| | |
|---|---|
| *design firm* | Engle + Murphy |
| *designer* | Robin Seaman |
| *client* | OnCall Healthcare Communications |
| *logo for* | Identity for company that provides demand management services to physicians and their patients by telephone. |

46.3

| | |
|---|---|
| *design firm* | Focus Design |
| *designers* | Brian Jacobson, Gustavo Alcantar |
| *art director* | Brian Jacobson |
| *illustrator* | Gustavo Alcantar |
| *client* | Inference Corporation |
| *logo for* | Event identity. |

47.1

| | |
|---|---|
| *design firm* | MJR Associates |
| *designer* | Frank Ruiz |
| *client* | Peter S. Levin MD |
| *logo for* | Corporate identity used on stationery, signage and marketing materials. |

47.2

| | |
|---|---|
| *design firm* | Alexander Atkins Design, Inc. |
| *designer* | Alexander Atkins |
| *client* | Lindstrom Represents |
| *logo for* | Company representing artists. |

47.3

| | |
|---|---|
| *design firm* | Alexander Atkins Design, Inc. |
| *designer* | Alexander Atkins |
| *client* | Stanford University |
| *logo for* | Women's conference focusing on business issues. |

47.04

| | |
|---|---|
| *design firm* | David Carter Graphic Design |
| *designer* | Emily Cain |
| *art director* | Lori Wilson |
| *client* | Disney Cruise Line |
| *logo for* | Common Grounds. |

47.1

47.2

47.3

47.4

After hours
OH BOY, A DESIGN COMPANY
5pm - 9am ®
Print Communications
OH BOY, A DESIGN COMPANY
Est. 1994 ®
Annual Reports
OH BOY, A DESIGN COMPANY
Est. 1994 ®
Advertising
OH BOY, A DESIGN COMPANY
Est. 1994 ®
Happy Holidays from
OH BOY, A DESIGN COMPANY
Est. 1994 ®
Branding and Identity
OH BOY, A DESIGN COMPANY
Est. 1994 ®

48.1

48.1

| | |
|---|---|
| *design firm* | Oh Boy, A Design Company |
| *designer* | Hunter L. Wimmer |
| *art director* | David Salanitro |
| *client* | Oh Boy, A Design Company |
| *logo for* | Self-promotion, business papers. |

49.1

| | |
|---|---|
| *design firm* | Solution 111 Design |
| *designer* | Darryl Glass |
| *client* | Custom Auto |
| *logo for* | Signage, stationery, van for auto shop that builds custom cars and engines. |

49.2

| | |
|---|---|
| *design firm* | Dutch Design |
| *designer* | Rick Smits |
| *client* | Dutch Design |
| *logo for* | Self-promotion. |

49.3

| | |
|---|---|
| *design firm* | Sandy Gin Design |
| *designer* | Sandy Gin |
| *client* | Sony Signatures |
| *logo for* | Proposed logo for a band. |

*49.1*

*49.2*

*49.3*

50.1

50.2

50.3

50.4

50.1

| | |
|---|---|
| *design firm* | Deluxe |
| *designer* | Tor Naerheim |
| *client* | Deluxe Brand |
| *logo for* | In-house Deluxe Brand identity. |

50.2

| | |
|---|---|
| *design firm* | GDS Studio |
| *designer* | Gary Solomon |
| *client* | The Creative Department.com |
| *logo for* | Image identity, stationery, website, T-shirts. |

50.3

| | |
|---|---|
| *design firm* | Sandy Gin Design |
| *designer* | Sandy Gin |
| *client* | Campusworks |
| *logo for* | An on-line textbook retailer. |

50.4

| | |
|---|---|
| *design firm* | Engle + Murphy |
| *designer* | Enily Moe |
| *client* | WisePlace |
| *logo for* | Corporate ID for organization that provides transitional services to homeless women. |

51.1

| | |
|---|---|
| *design firm* | The Huge Idea |
| *designer* | Lesli Wuco-B |
| *client* | Etudes |
| *logo for* | Distance education website. |

51.2

| | |
|---|---|
| *design firm* | Vigon/Ellis |
| *designer* | Marc Yeh |
| *art director* | Larry Vigon |
| *client* | BrainCo |
| *logo for* | Corporate identity. |

51.3

| | |
|---|---|
| *design firm* | Kevin Akers Designs |
| *designer* | Kevin Akers |
| *client* | Kids Cuts |
| *logo for* | Children's hair cutting salon. |

51.1

51.2

51.3

DIGITAL COLOR SYSTEMS

52.1

COLOR WORKS
DIGITAL IMAGING CENTER

52.2

MATCHFRAME

52.3

*52.1*
*design firm* Juddesign
*designers* Hal Maynerd, Eric Watanabe
*art director* Patti Judd
*client* Digital Color Systems
*logo for* Full service color house.

*52.2*
*design firm* Evolution Design
*art director* Bear Files
*client* Color Works
*logo for* Corporate identity for a color copy house in San Diego.

*52.3*
*design firm* Boardwalk
*designer* Harriet Breitborde
*client* Match Frame
*logo for* Marketing, promotion, signage.

*53.1*
*design firm* Moonlight Design
*designer* Karen Ryan
*art director* David Ryer
*client* Movietown.com
*logo for* Parent corporation of website selling VHS & DVD movies.

*53.2*
*design firm* The Wecker Group
*designer* Robert Wecker
*client* Delta Point, Inc.
*logo for* Packaging.

*53.3*
*design firm* Focus Design
*designer* Brian Jacobson
*client* Spectrum Photographic & Images
*logo for* Corporate identity.

*53.4*
*design firm* Zamboo
*designer* Dave Zambotti
*client* Z Filmmaker
*logo for* Independent film editor.

*53.5*
*design firm* Klass Design
*designer* Logo Doctor
*illustrator* Teri Klass
*client* Title House
*logo for* Proposed identity for a production house in Los Angeles.

*53.6*
*design firm* Michael Osborne Design
*designer* Paul Kagiwada
*art director* Michael Osborne
*client* Kelmscott Communications
*logo for* Printer.

53.1

53.2

53.3

53.4

53.5

53.6

54.1

Phil Rudy

Photography

54.2

CREATIVE STUDIO IMAGES

digital product photography

54.3

54.4

PAPPAS | TELEPRODUCTIONS

54.5

*54.1*
*design firm* Kevin Akers Designs
*designer* Kevin Akers
*client* Elapse Photo
*logo for* Film/photo developing store.

*54.2*
*design firm* Shields Design
*designer* Charles Shields
*illustrator* Phil Rudy
*client* Phil Rudy Photography
*logo for* Photographer.

*54.3*
*design firm* Jon Briggs Design
*designer* Jon Briggs
*client* Creative Studio Images
*logo for* Conveying company's identity and capabilities in the field of digital product photography.

*54.4*
*design firm* Akers Designs
*designer* Kevin Akers
*client* Friends of Photography
*logo for* Golf tournament.

*54.5*
*design firm* MJR Associates
*designer* Frank Ruiz
*client* Pappas Teleproductions
*logo for* Corporate identity used on stationery, signage and marketing materials.

*55.1*
*design firm* David Carter Graphic Design
*designer* Rickey Brown
*art director* Lori Wilson
*client* Disney Cruise Line
*logo for* Animator's Palate.

*55.2*
*design firm* Kevin Akers Designs
*designer* Kevin Akers
*client* Sharpe Models
*logo for* Talent agency.

*55.3*
*design firm* Fuse
*designer* Russell Pierce
*client* Joe Photo
*logo for* Corporate identity/brand.

*55.1*

*55.2*

*55.3*

56.1

56.2

56.3

56.1

| | |
|---|---|
| *design firm* | Susan Meshberg Graphic Design |
| *designer* | Susan Meshberg |
| *illustrators* | Elaine MacFarlane, Jia Hwang |
| *client* | Chateau Los Boldos |
| *logo for* | Trademark/identity for Chateau Los Boldos, a Chilean winery. |

56.2

| | |
|---|---|
| *design firm* | The Wecker Group |
| *designer* | Robert Wecker |
| *client* | Morgan Winery |
| *logo for* | Labels, packaging, stationery. |

56.3

| | |
|---|---|
| *design firm* | The Wecker Group |
| *designer* | Robert Wecker |
| *client* | Morgan Winery |
| *logo for* | Alternate logo. |

57.1

| | |
|---|---|
| *design firm* | The Wecker Group |
| *designer* | Robert Wecker |
| *client* | Valeria Winery |
| *logo for* | Packaging. |

57.2

| | |
|---|---|
| *design firm* | Jason Graham |
| *designer* | Jason Graham |
| *client* | La Bella Luna |
| *logo for* | Northern Italian Cuisine with an extensive wine list, accompanied by a romantic atmosphere. |

57.3

| | |
|---|---|
| *design firm* | Kevin Akers Designs |
| *designer* | Kevin Akers |
| *client* | Judee inc. |
| *logo for* | Holiday party. |

57.4

| | |
|---|---|
| *design firm* | David Carter Graphic Design |
| *designer* | Gary LoBue |
| *art director* | Lori Wilson |
| *client* | Disney Cruise Line |
| *logo for* | Palo. |

57.1

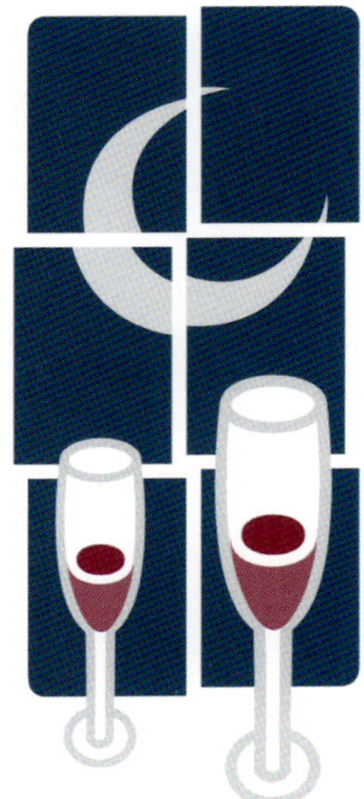

57.2

57.3

57.4

58.1

58.2

58.3

58.1
*design firm* McElveney & Palozzi Design Group, Inc.
*designer* Ellen Johnson
*art directors* William McElveney, Steve Palozzi
*client* Upstate Farms, Inc.
*logo for* Beverage labels, P.O.P. displays and banners.

58.2
*design firm* Primo Angeli Inc.
*designers* Sarah Sandstrom, Sandy Russell
*art director* Rich Scheve
*client* Crystal Geyser Water Company
*logo for* Jui2ce.

58.3
*design firm* Primo Angeli Inc.
*designers* Harumi Kubo, Koji Miyaki
*art directors* Rich Scheve
*client* Paramount Farms
*logo for* Fruit Rolls.

59.1
*design firm* The Wecker Group
*designer* Robert Wecker
*client* Café Au Lait Restaurant
*logo for* Signage, stationery.

59.2
*design firm* Blanco Design
*designer* Shelly Blanco
*client* Mother Mudd's Coffee

59.3
*design firm* David Carter Graphic Design
*designer* Tien Pham
*art director* Lori Wilson
*logo for* Sushi Sake

59.4
*design firm* Alexander Atkins Design, Inc.
*designer* Alexander Atkins
*client* Skinny Sippin
*logo for* Upscale fruit juice retailer.

59.5
*design firm* Kevin Akers Designs
*designer* Kevin Akers
*client* Baskin Robbins
*logo for* Internal team-building seminar.

Café Au Lait
coffee specialties and gourmet dishes
carmel-by-the-sea, california

59.1

Mother Mudd's

59.2

SUSHI SAKE

59.3

SKiNNY SiPPiN

59.4

59.5

Fowler Farms

60.1

Atwater Foods, INC.
Premium Dried Fruit

60.2

MAYER BROS.
Since 1852
FINE BEVERAGES

60.3

GREENE & HEMLY

60.4

60.5

60.1
*design firm* McElveney & Palozzi Design Group, Inc.
*designer* Jan Marie Gallagher
*art directors* William McElveney, Matt Nowicki
*client* Fowler Farms
*logo for* Letterhead, business cards, envelopes.

60.2
*design firm* McElveney & Palozzi Design Group, Inc.
*art directors* William McElveney, Lisa Williamson
*client* Atwater Foods, Inc.
*logo for* Letterhead, business cards, envelopes, brochure, sell sheets, website.

60.3
*design firm* McElveney & Palozzi Design Group, Inc.
*art director* William McElveney, Lisa Parenti
*client* Mayer Bros.
*logo for* Beverage labels, sell sheets, containment folder.

60.4
*design firm* MJR Associates
*designer* Frank Ruiz
*client* Greene & Hemly
*logo for* Corporate identity used on stationery, signage and marketing materials.

60.5
*design firm* Stone Yamashita
*designer* Jennifer Olsen
*client* David Binder Productions
*logo for* Theater producer in New York.

61.1
*design firm* Karen Mehoff & Co.
*designer* Karen Mehoff
*client* Apple Mountain Pie Company
*logo for* Identity for a home-baked pie company.

61.2
*design firm* Juddesign
*designers* Rosemary Rae, Karen Winward
*art director* Patti Judd
*client* California Avocado Category Marketing
*logo for* Avocado industry marketing association.

61.3
*design firm* Sandy Gin Design
*designer* Sandy Gin
*client* it's all good
*logo for* An upscale catering company.

*61.1*

*61.2*

*61.3*

JUST
SOUP
STEWS & CHILI TOO

62.1

VOTE FOR CAFFE CARDINALE
Carmel
BY-THE-SEA
Soup Election
WARNING – DO NOT CONSUME WITHIN CITY LIMITS

62.2

*62.1*
*design firm* Bryan Friel Studio
*designer* Bryan Friel
*client* Just Soup
*logo for* Signage, menus, ads.

*62.2*
*design firm* The Wecker Group
*designer* Robert Wecker
*client* Caffe Cardinale
*logo for* T-shirts, posters.

*63.1*
*design firm* Leeson Design
*designer* Susan Leeson
*client* BBQ Buddies
*logo for* A barbecue retail company that sells utensils, sauce, and everything else for the grill.

*63.2*
*design firm* Dutch Design
*designer* Rick Smits
*client* Lansing Christian School
*logo for* T-shirts and flyers.

*63.3*
*design firm* Allen Orr
*designer* Allen Orr
*client* Spud's Lounge

*63.1*

*63.2*

*63.3*

64.1

64.2

64.3

*64.1*

| | |
|---|---|
| *design firm* | David Carter Graphic Design |
| *designer* | Tien Pham |
| *art director* | Lori Wilson |
| *client* | Paris Resort and Casino |
| *logo for* | JJ's Boulangerie/Las Vegas, Nevada. |

*64.2*

| | |
|---|---|
| *design firm* | Taber Integrative Design |
| *designer* | Michele Taber |
| *client* | A Catered Affair: Hoagies Food & Beverage |
| *logo for* | The catering division of Hoagies Food & Beverage Corp. serving the Silicon Valley. |

*64.3*

| | |
|---|---|
| *design firm* | Lamfers & Associates |
| *designer* | Debra Lamfers |
| *illustrator* | Rose Cassano |
| *client* | Jessie et Laurent Culinary Service |
| *logo for* | Company identity—applied to print, signage and electronic media. |

*65.1*

| | |
|---|---|
| *design firm* | David Carter Graphic Design |
| *designer* | Emily Cain |
| *art director* | Lori Wilson |
| *client* | Portifino Bay Hotel |
| *logo for* | Splendido Pizzeria/Orlando, Florida. |

*65.2*

| | |
|---|---|
| *design firm* | The Wecker Group |
| *designer* | Robert Wecker |
| *client* | California Restaurant Association |
| *logo for* | Stationery. |

*65.3*

| | |
|---|---|
| *design firm* | Wallace Church Associates, Inc. |
| *designer* | Wendy Church |
| *illustrator* | Tracy Sabin |
| *client* | Mazola |
| *logo for* | Mazola pro chef cooking spray. |

SPLENDIDO PIZZERIA

65.1

CALIFORNIA
RESTAURANT
ASSOCIATION
EDUCATIONAL
FOUNDATION

65.2

65.3

66.1

66.2

66.3

*66.1*
*design firm* The Wecker Group
*designer* Robert Wecker
*client* City of Monterey
*logo for* Signage, stationery, collateral.

*66.2*
*design firm* McElveney & Palozzi Design Group, Inc.
*art directors* William McElveney, Jon Westfall
*client* CPI Business Groups
*logo for* Letterhead, business cards, envelopes, brochure.

*66.3*
*design firm* Elixir Design
*designer* Nathan Durrant
*art director* Jennifer Jerde
*illustrator* Nathan Durrant
*client* Earth Island Institute
*logo for* Non-profit environmental organization acting as an incubator for projects promoting conservation, preservation, and restoration of the earth.

*67.1*
*design firm* GDS Studio
*designer* Gary Solomon
*client* Daniels Financial Services
*logo for* Stationery system and press kit.

*67.2*
*design firm* Shields Design
*designer* Charles Shields
*client* Main Street Trading Company
*logo for* Investments company.

*67.3*
*design firm* Stoyan Design
*designer* Michael Stinson
*art director* David Wooters
*illustrator* Michael Stinson
*client* Cytovia

*67.4*
*design firm* Focus Design
*designer* Brian Jacobson
*client* Ösel Incorporated
*logo for* Corporate identity.

*67.5*
*design firm* Stoyan Design
*designer* Michael Stinson
*client* Global Technology Distribution Council

*67.6*
*design firm* The Wecker Group
*designer* Robert Wecker
*client* The Wecker Group
*logo for* Signage, stationery, forms.

67.1

Newhall
DISCOUNT
Futures & Options

67.2

CYTOVIA

67.3

ÖSEL

67.4

67.5

theweckergroup
ADVERTISING DESIGN

67.6

68.1

68.2

68.3

68.1

| | |
|---|---|
| *design firm* | Solution 111 Design |
| *designer* | Darryl Glass |
| *client* | Global Web |
| *logo for* | Advertising for a website developer and host. |

68.2

| | |
|---|---|
| *design firm* | Fuse |
| *designer* | Russell Pierce |
| *client* | PairGain (Open Planet) |
| *logo for* | Promotional program, used in advertising and signage. |

68.3

| | |
|---|---|
| *design firm* | Sandy Gin Design |
| *designer* | Sandy Gin |
| *client* | Origin Medsystems |
| *logo for* | An in-house use at a medical device company. |

69.1

| | |
|---|---|
| *design firm* | Moonlight Design |
| *designer* | David Ryer |
| *client* | Sci-Fi Universe Magazine |
| *logo for* | Annual awards honoring science fiction books, films, TV, etc. |

69.2

| | |
|---|---|
| *design firm* | McElveney & Palozzi Design Group, Inc. |
| *art directors* | Steve Palozzi, Jon Westfall |
| *client* | Auto-Soft |
| *logo for* | Brochure, sell sheets, software packaging for Material Control Rx. |

69.3

| | |
|---|---|
| *design firm* | Moonlight Design |
| *designer* | David Ryer |
| *client* | WorldTel |
| *logo for* | Company selling prepaid phone service cards. |

69.4

| | |
|---|---|
| *design firm* | The Wecker Group |
| *designer* | Robert Wecker |
| *client* | Monterey Network Center |
| *logo for* | Signage, stationery, collateral. |

69.5

| | |
|---|---|
| *design firm* | McElveney & Palozzi Design Group, Inc. |
| *designer* | Dillon Constable |
| *art directors* | William McElveney, Matt Nowicki |
| *client* | G-Force Collaborations |
| *logo for* | Letterhead, business cards, envelopes. |

69.6

| | |
|---|---|
| *design firm* | The Wecker Group |
| *designer* | Robert Wecker |
| *client* | OnLine Interpreters |
| *logo for* | Signage, stationery, forms, collateral. |

Sci-Fi Universe Readers' Choice
Universe Awards

69.1

MATERIAL Rx CONTROL

69.2

WORLDtel

69.3

MNC
MONTEREY NETWORK CENTER

69.4

G-FORCE
COLLABORATIONS

69.5

OnLine Interpreters
The Global Connection

69.6

70.1

70.2

70.3

*70.1*
*design firm* Lewis Design
*art director* June Lewis
*illustrator* Tracy Sabin
*client* Kidcare Express
*logo for* Healthcare informational bus for public schools.

*70.2*
*design firm* Kevin Akers Designs
*designer* Kevin Akers
*client* San Francisco Symphony
*logo for* New Year's Eve 2000 gala concert.

*70.3*
*design firm* Shields Design
*designer* Laura Thornton
*art director* Charles Shields
*client* Children's Hospital
*logo for* Hospital program.

*71.1*
*design firm* ComCorp, Inc.
*designer* ComCorp Staff
*art director* George Kubricht
*client* Kartoon Kingdom
*logo for* Retail marketing collateral.

*71.2*
*design firm* Sandy Gin Design
*designer* Sandy Gin
*client* Fila Footwear
*logo for* Proposed logo for use on clothing line.

*71.3*
*design firm* Mike Salisbury Communications
*art director* Mike Salisbury
*illustrator* Dave Parmely
*client* Paramount
*logo for* Phantom.

*71.4*
*design firm* The Wecker Group
*designer* Robert Wecker
*client* Hot Wax Media
*logo for* Stationery.

*71.5*
*design firm* BobCo Design Inc.
*designer* Robert S. Nenninger
*client* Bandai America
*logo for* Packaging for a line of pocket-sized toys called "Virtual Pets." These toys started a revolution.

*71.6*
*design firm* BobCo Design Inc.
*designer* Robert S. Nenninger
*client* Bandai America
*logo for* Packaging for a line of "Virtual Pet" toys that are connected together to battle each other.

71.1

71.2

71.3

71.4

71.5

71.6

Adamm's

STAINED GLASS & AMERICAN CRAFT GALLERY

72.1

the Body Exclusive

72.2

Celebrity™

72.3

*72.1*
*design firm* Innovative Design and Advertising
*designers* Susan Nickey-Newton, Kim Crossett-Neumann
*illustrator* Dan Cotton
*client* Adamm's Stained Glass
*logo for* Signage, business cards, letterhead, gift bags.

*72.2*
*design firm* Vigon/Ellis
*designer* Brian Jackson
*art director* Larry Vigon
*client* Body Exclusive
*logo for* Corporate identity.

*72.3*
*design firm* The Marketing Store
*designer* Kevin Wilhelm
*client* Altaireyewear
*logo for* Celebrity eyewear.

*75.1*
*design firm* Jeffry Hipp
*designer* Jeffry Hipp
*client* National Ford Tool Collectors
*logo for* National club for collectors of Ford automobile tools. Identity system.

*73.2*
*design firm* Mike Salisbury Communications
*designers* Mike Salisbury, Brian Sisson
*art director* Dave Willardson
*illustrator* Bob Maile
*client* Hasbro

*73.3*
*design firm* Stephgrafx
*designer* Stephanie Payan
*client* Talking Hearts Press
*logo for* Book publisher and public speaker.

*73.4*
*design firm* Primo Angeli Inc.
*designers* Terrence Tong, Oscar Mulder
*art director* Jennifer Bethke
*client* Sara Lee
*logo for* Sara Lee.

*73.1*

*73.2*

*73.3*

*73.4*

THE Paragon FOUNDATION

74.1

Get Creative™

74.2

Walter Dyer's
SHOES & LEATHER

74.3

FLOWER HILL
Flowers

74.4

Lauren Meyer Communications, Inc.

74.5

*74.1*
*design firm* Juddesign
*designer* Eric Watanabe
*art director* Patti Judd
*client* The Paragon Foundation
*logo for* Mission value management organization.

*74.2*
*design firm* GDS Studio
*designer* Gary Solomon
*client* Vivitar Corporation
*logo for* Ad campaign and point-of-purchase for home digital art studio, promoting digital camera, scanner, printer for the whole family.

*74.3*
*design firm* McElveney & Palozzi Design Group, Inc.
*designer* Paul Reisinger, Jr.
*art director* Matt Nowicki
*client* Walter Dyer's Shoes & Leather
*logo for* Direct mail pieces.

*74.4*
*design firm* Minka Willig Design
*designer* Minka Willig
*xclient* Flower Hill Flowers
*logo for* Flower shop identity system.

*74.5*
*design firm* Eve Vrla Design
*designer* Eve Vrla
*client* Lauren Meyer Communications, Inc.
*logo for* Corporate identity event planning and marketing firm.

*75.1*
*design firm* Conover
*designer* Melissa Fraser
*art director* David Conover
*client* Shea Homes
*logo for* Residential home development.

*75.2*
*design firm* Portal Publications
*designer* Mabel Shiue
*art director* Gary Higgins
*client* Portal Publications
*logo for* A greeting card line called "wise little souls" to send the message that our children, perfect from birth, are both our students and our teachers.

*5.3*
*design firm* VWA Group
*designer* Brian Blankenship
*art director* Rhonda Warren
*client* Jefferson Property, Inc.
*logo for* Identity, letterhead, brochure, advertisements for Jefferson at LaValencia.

TorreyView

*75.1*

PORTAL'S

wise little souls

*75.2*

Jefferson at LaValencia

Premier Apartment Homes

*75.3*

HORIZONS
THE LODGE AT WOODCLIFF

76.1

THE LODGE AT
Woodcliff

76.2

maltwhiskey.com

76.3

Hammerheads
A GASTRONOMICAL EXPERIENCE

76.4

*76.1*
*design firm* McElveney & Palozzi Design Group, Inc.
*art directors* William McElveney, Ellen Johnson
*client* The Lodge at Woodcliff
*logo for* Horizons restaurant menus.

*76.2*
*design firm* McElveney & Palozzi Design Group, Inc.
*art directors* William McElveney, Ellen Johnson
*client* The Lodge at Woodcliff
*logo for* Letterhead, business cards, envelopes, brochure, signage.

*6.3*
*design firm* Shields Design
*designer* Charles Shields
*illustrator* Camerad
*client* Malt Whiskey.com
*logo for* Website.

*76.4*
*design firm* The Wecker Group
*designers* Robert Wecker, Mark Savee
*client* Hammerheads Restaurant
*logo for* Signage, menus, specialty advertising.

*77.1*
*design firm* Curry Design Associates
*designer* Jason Scheideman
*client* Curioso
*logo for* Specialty boutique store.

*77.2*
*design firm* Klass Design
*designer* Logo Doctor
*art director* Teri Klass
*illustrator* Tim Clark
*client* Optimism
*logo for* Identity for a fragrance company.

*77.3*
*design firm* David Carter Graphic Design
*designer* Tabitha Bogard
*art director* Lori Wilson
*client* Paris Resort and Casino
*logo for* Du Parc/Las Vegas, Nevada.

*77.4*
*design firm* David Carter Graphic Design
*designer* Sharon LeJeune
*art director* Lori Wilson
*client* Mandalay Bay Resort and Casino
*logo for* Shanghai Lilly/Las Vegas, Nevada.

Curioso

*77.1*

Optimism

*77.2*

du PARC

*77.3*

SHANGHAI LILLY

*77.4*

78.1

| | |
|---|---|
| *design firm* | M Studio |
| *designer* | Mabel Shiue |
| *client* | Blow Fish-Sushi To Die For |
| *logo for* | A cutting-edge restaurant with focus on bar, sushi and loud music. |

78.2

| | |
|---|---|
| *design firm* | Klass Design |
| *designer* | Logo Doctor |
| *art director* | Stephen Noriega |
| *illustrator* | Teri Klass |
| *client* | Cava Restaurant |
| *logo for* | Identity for a night club. |

78.3

| | |
|---|---|
| *design firm* | The Wecker Group |
| *designer* | Robert Wecker |
| *client* | Kazu Public Radio |
| *logo for* | Wine tasting fund raiser, programs. |

79.1

| | |
|---|---|
| *design firm* | MJR Associates |
| *designer* | Aimee McKirdy |
| *art director* | Frank Ruiz |
| *client* | California Sprouts |
| *logo for* | Corporate identity used on stationery, signage and marketing materials. |

79.2

| | |
|---|---|
| *design firm* | Innovative Design and Advertising |
| *designers* | Susan Nickey-Newton, Kim Crossett-Neumann |
| *client* | Markie D's Restaurant |
| *logo for* | Signage, flyers, menus, business cards, ads, etc. |

79.3

| | |
|---|---|
| *design firm* | The Wecker Group |
| *designer* | James Kyllo |
| *art director* | Robert Wecker |
| *client* | McAbee Beach Cafe |
| *logo for* | Signage, menus, stationery, specialty advertising. |

79.4

| | |
|---|---|
| *design firm* | The Wecker Group |
| *designers* | Ruth Minerva, Craig Rader |
| *art director* | Robert Wecker |
| *client* | Michael's Restaurant |
| *logo for* | Signage, stationery. |

78.1

78.2

78.3

CALIFORNIA
Sprouts

79.1

Markie D's
AMERICAN GRILLE

79.2

McABEE BEACH
Cafe

79.3

michael's
A RESTAURANT

79.4

80.1

80.2

80.3

80.1
*design firm* Kevin Akers Designs
*designer* Kevin Akers
*client* Kenwood Group
*logo for* Conference graphic.

80.2
*design firm* Tom Fowler, Inc.
*designer* Karl S. Maruyama
*client* St. Luke's LifeWorks
*logo for* An annual report whose theme was "What it takes to build a home."

80.3
*design firm* Zamboo
*designer* Dave Zambotti
*client* Big Sisters of Los Angeles
*logo for* Corporate identity.

81.1
*design firm* Focus Design
*designers* Brian Jacobson, Creighton Dinsmore
*client* Inference and Cybergold
*logo for* Special incentive program.

81.2
*design firm* Seaman Design Group/Sheppard & Assoc.
*designer* Robin Seaman
*client* Apple Computer, Inc.
*logo for* Their Environmental Health and Safety Program that encourages sound procedures, healthy living and safe working practices.

Cash 2 Register™

BY INFERENCE AND CYBERGOLD

81.1

81.2

82.1

82.2

82.3

82.1

| | |
|---|---|
| *design firm* | Seaman Design Group |
| *designer* | Robin Seaman |
| *client* | The California Endowment |
| *logo for* | A philanthropic foundation whose mission is to expand access to affordable, quality health care for the underserved communities of California. |

82.2

| | |
|---|---|
| *design firm* | The Huge Idea |
| *designer* | Lesli Wuco-B |
| *client* | For Pets' Sake.com |
| *logo for* | Company/Website. |

82.3

| | |
|---|---|
| *design firm* | Tom Fowler, Inc. |
| *designer* | Thomas G. Fowler |
| *client* | Ross Products Division/Abbott Laboratories |
| *logo for* | Creating a cohesive look to all the various resource materials and services Ross Products provides the pediatrics nursing industry. |

83.1

| | |
|---|---|
| *design firm* | Vigon/Ellis |
| *designer* | Brian Jackson |
| *art director* | Larry Vigon |
| *client* | Enfish Technology Inc. |
| *logo for* | Corporate identity. |

enfish®

83.1

Conner's Cause for Children

84.1

84.2

FRIENDS of SIGNAL HILL CULTURAL ARTS

84.3

84.1
*design firm* John Champ Design Associates
*designer* Randall Cohen
*art director* John Champ
*client* Conner's Cause for Children
*logo for* Non-profit organization's identity.

84.2
*design firm* Wolfback Design
*designer* Karin Scholz
*client* Stephen Miller Gallery
*logo for* Oriental rug gallery.

84.3
*design firm* Blanco Design
*designer* Shelly Blanco
*client* Friends of Signal Hill Cultural Arts

85.1
*design firm* Kevin Akers Designs
*designer* Kevin Akers
*client* Western Arts Alliance
*logo for* Entertainment promoter—family of logos developed for conference topics.

*85.1*

Art Therapy Institute
OF SAN FRANCISCO

86.1

WOMEN ACROSS GENERATIONS
...A Volounteer Resource

86.2

Rehabilitation
Providers

86.3

MONTEREY COUNTY
DEPARTMENT OF SOCIAL SERVICES

86.4

CABRINI-GREEN
Tutoring Program, Inc.

86.5

87.1

87.2

87.3

86.1
*design firm* Lamfers & Associates
*designer* Debra Lamfers
*illustrator* Linda Chapman
*client* Art Therapy Institute
*logo for* Company identity and applications. Art Therapy Institute helps children through art therapy and teaches medical professionals these skills.

86.2
*design firm* Benita Oberg Design
*designer* Benita Oberg
*client* Women Across Generations
*logo for* Stationery, collateral, web.

86.3
*design firm* The Wecker Group
*designer* Robert Wecker
*client* Rehabilitation Providers
*logo for* Signage, stationery, forms.

86.4
*design firm* The Wecker Group
*designer* Robert Wecker
*client* Monterey County Department of Social Services
*logo for* Stationery, signage.

86.5
*design firm* ComCorp, Inc.
*designer* Abby Mines
*client* Cabrini-Green Tutoring Program
*logo for* Corporate material and volunteer material.

87.1
*design firm* Stewart Monderer Design, Inc.
*designer* Stewart Monderer
*client* Health Quarters
*logo for* Identity.

87.2
*design firm* Lorenz
*designer* Arne Ratermanis
*client* Teen Life Choice
*logo for* Identity for a non-profit organization.

87.3
*design firm* J. Robert Faulkner Advertising
*designer* J. Robert Faulkner
*client* Equal Access

FRIEDLAND JACOBS

COMMUNICATIONS

88.1

RED BOY GEAR

88.2

CAM

SERVICES

COMMON AREA
MAINTENANCE

88.3

*88.1*
*design firm* Vigon/Ellis
*designer* Brian Jackson
*art director* Larry Vigon
*client* Friedland Jacobs Communications
*logo for* Corporate identity.

*88.2*
*design firm* Solution 111 Design
*designer* Darryl Glass
*client* Red Boy Gear
*logo for* Labels, sales tags and stationery for Red Boy Gear, a clothing manufacturer.

*88.3*
*design firm* Klass Design
*designer* Logo Doctor
*illustrator* Teri Klass
*client* CAM Services
*logo for* Identity for a maintenance company in Los Angeles.

*89.1*
*design firm* Klass Design
*designer* Logo Doctor
*art director* Teri Klass
*illustrator* Tim Clark
*client* Stock Exchange
*logo for* Identity for a night club in Los Angeles.

*89.2*
*design firm* Klass Design
*designer* Logo Doctor
*art directors* Tim Clark, Teri Klass
*illustrator* Teri Klass
*client* Bad Driver Productions
*logo for* Identity system for movie production company.

*89.3*
*design firm* The Gap
*designer* Logo Doctor
*art director* Tim Cohrs
*illustrator* Tim Clark
*client* The Gap Store
*logo for* The Gap Rap Magazine website.

*89.1*

*89.2*

*89.3*

90.1

90.2

90.3

90.1

| | |
|---|---|
| *design firm* | Talbot Design Group |
| *designer* | Chris Kosman |
| *art director* | GayLyn Talbot |
| *client* | MBK- My Brother's Keeper |
| *logo for* | Identity and collateral (stationery, labels, invitations). |

90.2

| | |
|---|---|
| *design firm* | Juddesign |
| *designer* | Steve Donegan |
| *art director* | Patti Judd |
| *client* | Freedom Carpet Care |
| *logo for* | Carpet cleaning service. |

90.3

| | |
|---|---|
| *design firm* | Carol Gravelle Graphic Design |
| *designer* | Carol Gravelle |
| *client* | Act Networks, Inc. |
| *logo for* | Company motivational materials. |

91.1

| | |
|---|---|
| *design firm* | Pierre Rademaker Design |
| *designer* | Pierre Rademaker, Jeff Austin |
| *client* | Hello Central |
| *logo for* | Print items, product catalogue. |

91.2

| | |
|---|---|
| *design firm* | Tsuchiya Sloneker Communications, Inc. |
| *designer* | Colin O'Neill |
| *art director* | Mark Sloneker |
| *illustrator* | Colin O'Neill |
| *client* | Eastman Kodak/Themed Entertainment |
| *logo for* | Service logo—product packaging. |

91.3

| | |
|---|---|
| *design firm* | Moonlight Design |
| *designer* | Karen Ryan |
| *art director* | David Ryer |
| *client* | CompletePT |
| *logo for* | Company providing land and aquatic physical therapy and rehab services. |

91.4

| | |
|---|---|
| *design firm* | MJR Associates |
| *designer* | Frank Ruiz |
| *client* | Stephen J. Ikemiya DDS |
| *logo for* | Corporate identity used on stationery, signage and marketing materials. |

91.5

| | |
|---|---|
| *design firm* | Bryan Friel Studio |
| *designer* | Bryan Friel |
| *client* | Melanie Crandall & Associates |
| *logo for* | Stationery, promotional items. |

HELLO CENTRAL
ANTIQUE TELEPHONE Co.

91.1

Kodak

91.2

CompletePT
POOL & LAND PHYSICAL THERAPY

91.3

Stephen J. Ikemiya, D.D.S.
Restorative, Esthetic and Implant Dentistry

91.4

91.5

*92.1*
*design firm* Mortensen Design
*designer* PJ Nidecker
*art director* Gordon Mortensen
*client* MyPlay, Inc.
*logo for* High-tech company.

*92.2*
*design firm* Mortensen Design
*designer* PJ Nidecker
*art director* Gordon Mortensen
*client* Handspring, Inc. (Springboard)
*logo for* High-tech company.

*92.3*
*design firm* Mortensen Design
*designer* PJ Nidecker
*art director* Gordon Mortensen
*client* Handspring, Inc.
*logo for* High-tech company.

*93.1*
*design firm* Michelle Leshner Designs
*designer* Michelle Leshner
*illustrator* Lise Dahms
*client* Fitness Plus
*logo for* Business system and all collateral materials.

*93.2*
*design firm* CTS Design
*designer* Claire T. Smith
*client* Kitafit
*logo for* Fitness videos and company identity.

*93.3*
*design firm* Carol Gravelle Graphic Design
*designer* Carol Gravelle
*art director* Paddy Farrell-Thomas
*illustrator* Carol Gravelle
*client* SourceCom
*logo for* Product for networking router.

*93.4*
*design firm* Prints of Peach Design Group
*designers* Warren Lloyd Dayton, Martha S. Dayton
*client* Jerry Blevins
*logo for* Letterhead, business card, invoice, for physical fitness trainer.

*93.5*
*design firm* Bryan Friel Studio
*designer* Bryan Friel
*client* The Sports Club/LA
*logo for* Signage, merchandise, corporate literature.

*92.1*

*92.2*

*92.3*

FITNESS PLUS

93.1

kitafit
defy gravity...

93.2

BATON

93.3

93.4

THE SPORTS CLUB/LA

93.5

94.1

94.2

94.3

94.1
design firm Carol Gravelle Graphic Design
designer Carol Gravelle
art director Barbara Mizuno
illustrator Carol Gravelle
client Camelbak
logo for Product featuring "hands free hydration" possible with Camelbak water system.

94.2
design firm Earlywine Design
designer Terry Earlywine
client Offset Fulfilment Services
logo for Company identity, stationery, signage.

94.3
design firm Stewart Monderer Design, Inc.
designer Aime Lecusay
art director Stewart Monderer
client Corporate Communications, Inc.
logo for Identity.

95.1
design firm The Huge Idea
designer Lesli Wuco-B
client Lesli Wuco-B
logo for Design studio.

95.2
design firm Alexander Atkins Design, Inc.
designer Alexander Atkins
client Abbott Usability
logo for Company that conducts product evaluations.

95.3
design firm Heart Times Coffee Cup Equals Lighting
designer Paul Rogers
art director Bobby Woods
illustrator Paul Rogers
client Seed Productions
logo for Film production company.

95.4
design firm Shields Design
designer Juan Vega
art director Charles Shields
client Attitude Online
logo for Internet service provider.

95.1

95.2

95.3

95.4

Black & Blu
ENTERTAINMENT

96.1

MUSIC CITY TICKETS

MUSIC CITY TICKETS

MUSIC CITY TICKETS

96.2

WINDCARE

96.3

97.1

97.2

97.3

*96.1*
*design firm* Zamboo
*designers* Jeff Allison, Becca Bootes
*client* Black & Blu Entertainment
*logo for* Corporate identity.

*96.2*
*design firm* Stone Yamashita
*designer* Jennifer Olsen
*client* City Tickets
*logo for* Ticket broker service for all kinds of events.

*96.3*
*design firm* Alexander Atkins Design, Inc.
*designer* Alexander Atkins
*client* Wind River Systems
*logo for* Technical support service.

*97.1*
*design firm* Bruce Yelaska Design
*designer* Bruce Yelaska
*client* Messenger Greeting Cards
*logo for* Whimsical line of greeting cards and accessories.

*97.2*
*design firm* Fuse
*designer* Matthew Stainer
*client* Direct Fit
*logo for* Overall corporate identity/brand, used in both print and digital mediums.

*97.3*
*design firm* Moonlight Design
*designer* Damon Seeley
*art director* David Ryer
*client* The Max Agency
*logo for* A boutique ad agency.

*98.1*
*design firm* Earlywine Design
*designer* Terry Earlywine
*client* The Earlywine Family Crest
*logo for* Wine box labels.

*98.2*
*design firm* MJR Associates
*designer* Frank Ruiz
*client* Navmed
*logo for* Corporate identity used on stationery and marketing materials.

*98.3*
*design firm* Kevin Akers Designs
*designer* Kevin Akers
*client* Kevin Akers Designs
*logo for* Design studio.

*99.1*
*design firm* Hennelly Design Office
*designer* Barbara Hennelly
*client* Hennelly Design Office
*logo for* Graphic designer business system application.

*99.2*
*design firm* CKS Partners (Cupertino, CA)
*designer* Barbara Hennelly
*art director* Mike Bohrer
*client* Evoke

*99.3*
*design firm* Karen Mehoff & Co.
*designer* Karen Mehoff
*client* Pacific Power Systems, LLC
*logo for* Company identity for an electrical systems integrator.

*99.4*
*design firm* Stewart Monderer Design, Inc.
*designer* Stewart Monderer
*client* Kallix Corporation
*logo for* Identity.

*99.5*
*design firm* Shimokochi/Reeves
*designer* Mamoru Shimokochi
*client* Zig Ziglar Network Trademark
*logo for* Corporate identity program.

*99.6*
*design firm* John Champ Design Associates
*designer* Randall Cohen
*art director* John Champ
*client* Certus International Incorporated
*logo for* Corporate identity.

*98.1*

*98.2*

*98.3*

99.1

99.2

kallix

99.3

99.4

ZIG ZIGLAR NETWORK

99.5

99.6

BURKE WILLIAMS

100.1

SonicSource™
CORPORATION

100.2

COREVENT

100.3

DentalAdvantage™

100.4

ALWAYS AN ANSWER

100.5

101.1

M. Hurt Supply, Ltd.

101.2

ADLINK®

101.3

*100.1*
*design firm* Shimokochi/Reeves
*designer* Mamoru Shimokochi
*art director* Anne Reeves
*client* Burke Williams
*logo for* Branding identity & packaging system.

*100.2*
*design firm* Shields Design
*designer* Laura Thornton
*art director* Charles Shields
*client* SonicSource
*logo for* E-commerce.

*100.3*
*design firm* Engle + Murphy
*designer* Mark Sojka
*client* Corevent
*logo for* Corporate ID for company that handles marketing and design for corporate-sponsored sports events.

*100.4*
*design firm* Moonlight Design
*designer* David Ryer
*client* Dental Advantage
*logo for* Company providing consulting, financial and education services to dentists.

*100.5*
*design firm* Lawless Graphic Design
*designer* John P. Lawless
*client* Always An Answer
*logo for* Financial consulting firm specializing in seeking solutions for foreclosure and bankruptcy prevention.

*101.1*
*design firm* Miriello Grafico, Inc.
*designer* Chris Keeney, Dennis Garcia
*client* Newport Communications

*101.2*
*design firm* Lawless Graphic Design
*designer* John P. Lawless
*client* M. Hurt Supply, Ltd.
*logo for* Plumbing and electrical supply wholesaler.

*101.3*
*design firm* Vigon/Ellis
*designer* Brian Jackson
*art director* Larry Vigon
*client* Adlink
*logo for* Corporate identity.

102.1
*design firm* Stewart Monderer Design, Inc.
*designer* Stewart Monderer Design
*client* Dynisco, Inc.
*logo for* Identity.

102.2
*design firm* Earlywine Design
*designer* Terry Earlywine
*client* Stepping Stones
*logo for* Identity, stationery, signage and trucks for landscaping company.

102.3
*design firm* Zamboo
*designers* Becca Bootes, Chris Go
*art director* Dave Zambotti
*client* Demand Software
*logo for* Corporate identity.

103.1
*design firm* Lorenz
*designer* Arne Ratermanis
*client* Holocomm Systems, Inc.
*logo for* Company identity.

103.2
*design firm* Calori & Vanden-Eynden
*designers* Denise Funaro, Jordan Marcus
*art director* Chris Calori
*client* DC Heritage Tourism Coalition
*logo for* Marker of historical districts and trails in Washington, DC.

103.3
*design firm* Stewart Monderer Design, Inc.
*designer* Aime Lecusay
*art director* Stewart Monderer
*client* NBase/Xyplex
*logo for* Identity.

103.4
*design firm* Shimokochi/Reeves
*designer* Mamoru Shimokochi
*art director* Anne Reeves
*client* Beverly Sassoon International
*logo for* Branding identity & packaging system/ specialty skin care.

103.5
*design firm* Vigon/Ellis
*designer* Brian Jackson
*art director* Larry Vigon
*client* Employers Group
*logo for* Corporate identity.

102.1

102.2

102.3

HOLOCOMM™
SYSTEMS INC

103.1

103.2

103.3

BEVERLY
SASSOON

103.4

employers
group *People & Productivity*

103.5

104.1

104.2

104.3

104.1
*design firm* McElveney & Palozzi Design Group, Inc.
*art director* Steve Palozzi
*client* Spring Street Society

104.2
*design firm* David Carter Graphic Design
*designer* Emily Cain
*art director* Lori Wilson
*client* Abacus Restaurant
*logo for* Restaurant in Dallas, Texas.

104.3
*design firm* Calori & Vanden-Eynden
*designer* Denise Funaro
*art director* Chris Calori
*client* Fulton Street Mall
*logo for* Business Improvement District. Urban shopping area in Brooklyn, NY.

105.1
*design firm* Stephgrafx
*designer* Stephanie Payan
*client* Nuvonix Interactive
*logo for* Website company.

105.2
*design firm* Deluxe Brand
*designer* Tor Naerheim
*client* ARDEO
*logo for* Corporate identity for manufacturer of fire retardant products.

105.3
*design firm* Vigon/Ellis
*designer* Marc Yeh
*art director* Larry Vigon
*client* Eteamz
*logo for* Corporate identity.

105.4
*design firm* Communications Design
*designer* Susan Leeson
*art director* Bill Sykes
*client* Advanced Technology Staffing
*logo for* Technology staffing agency for high-end programmers.

105.5
*design firm* Vigon/Ellis
*designers* Marc Yeh, Brian Jackson
*art director* Larry Vigon
*client* Gravity Games
*logo for* Corporate identity.

nuvonix
interactive

105.1

ARDEO®
fire systems

105.2

eteamz

105.3

105.4

GRAVITY™
GAMES

105.5

*106.1*
*design firm* Dutch Design
*designer* Rick Smits
*client* LRH Management
*logo for* Business cards.

*106.2*
*design firm* Bryan Friel Studio
*designer* Bryan Friel
*client* Manhattan Country Club
*logo for* Signage, corporate literature.

*106.3*
*design firm* Wolfback Design
*designer* Karin Scholz
*client* Synapse
*logo for* Corporate ID for Internet connectivity consultants.

*107.1*
*design firm* Eve Vrla Design
*designer* Eve Vrla
*client* Trucenna Enterprises
*logo for* Corporate identity, stationery and signage for general contractor.

*107.2*
*design firm* Earlywine Design
*designer* Terry Earlywine
*client* Massage at the Mansion
*logo for* Company identity, stationery, signage.

*107.3*
*design firm* Conover
*designer* David Conover
*client* Fraseworks
*logo for* Educational assessment firm.

*107.4*
*design firm* Seaman Design Group
*designer* Robin Seaman
*client* Typecraft, Inc.
*logo for* A printer with a technical edge over the competition, They wanted to communicate their leading position in the market.

*107.5*
*design firm* John Champ Design Associates
*designer* Randall Cohen
*art director* John Champ
*client* Quidel Corporation
*logo for* Sales incentive program.

*106.1*

*106.2*

*106.3*

TRUCENNA

107.1

107.2

107.3

107.4

ascend

107.5

108.1

108.2

matinee
ENTERTAINMENT

108.3

BALDWIN
PRODUCTIONS

108.4

ereel

108.5

VANSCOY

108.6

PERSPECTA

09.1

EPLOYMENT

109.2

PALM COMPUTING PLATFORM

109.3

*108.1*
*design firm* Curry Design Associates
*designer* Steve Curry
*client* Muse X Editions
*logo for* Digital fine art printing company.

*108.2*
*design firm* Kevin Akers Designs
*designer* Kevin Akers
*client* Susan Sargent Designs
*logo for* Textile designer.

*108.3*
*design firm* Vigon/Ellis
*designer* Marc Yeh
*art director* Larry Vigon
*client* Matinee Entertainment
*logo for* Corporate identity.

*108.4*
*design firm* Vigon/Ellis
*designer* Marc Yeh
*art director* Larry Vigon
*client* Baldwin Productions
*logo for* Corporate identity.

*108.5*
*design firm* Vigon/Ellis
*designer* Marc Yeh
*art director* Larry Vigon
*client* Ereel
*logo for* Corporate identity.

*108.6*
*design firm* Curry Design Associates
*designer* Jason Scheideman
*client* Vanscoy
*logo for* Photographer.

*109.1*
*design firm* Elixir Design
*designer* Nathan Durrant
*art director* Jennifer Jerde
*client* Perspecta Inc.
*logo for* Company has created software enabling users to organize and navigate information in a simulated, multi-dimensional web space.

*109.2*
*design firm* Vigon/Ellis
*designer* Marc Yeh
*art director* Larry Vigon
*client* Eployment
*logo for* Corporate identity.

*109.3*
*design firm* Mortensen Design
*designer* Wendy Chon
*art director* Gordon Mortensen
*client* Hewlett-Packard (Palm computing)
*logo for* High-tech company.

*110.1*
*design firm* GSD Studio
*designer* Gary Solomon
*client* Mosaic
*logo for* Retail advertising and marketing Identity of all promotional items, website.

*110.2*
*design firm* Seaman Design Group
*designer* Robin Seaman
*client* Hope, Hispanas Organized for Political Equality
*logo for* Non-profit organization established to further the education and participation of Latina women in the political process.

*110.3*
*design firm* Mike Salisbury Communications
*designer* Logo Doctor
*art director* Mike Salisbury
*illustrator* Tim Clark
*client* Mike Salisbury
*logo for* Identity for a car dealership.

*111.1*
*design firm* Mortensen Design
*designer* PJ Nidecker
*art director* Gordon Mortensen
*client* Mirapoint, Inc.
*logo for* High-tech company.

*111.2*
*design firm* Stoyan Design
*designer* Michael Stinson
*client* Bell Photography

*111.3*
*design firm* Vigon/Ellis
*designer* Brian Jackson
*art director* Larry Vigon
*client* Air Creative Group
*logo for* Corporate identity.

*111.4*
*design firm* Sabingrafik, Inc.
*designer* Tracy Sabin
*illustrator* Tracy Sabin
*client* Tom Stacey
*logo for* A copywriter.

*110.1*

*110.2*

*110.3*

MIRAPOINT

111.1

111.2

AIR CREATIVE GROUP

111.3

the Wordsmith

111.4

112.1

112.2

112.3

112.4

112.1

| | |
|---|---|
| *design firm* | Zamboo |
| *designer* | Dave Zambotti |
| *art director* | Becca Bootes |
| *client* | Creative Management Coordinators |
| *logo for* | Corporate identity. |

112.2

| | |
|---|---|
| *design firm* | Lamfers & Associates |
| *designer* | Missy Nery |
| *art director* | Debra Lamfers |
| *client* | News Printing Company, Inc. |
| *logo for* | Company identity and applications for a printer specializing in newspaper production. |

112.3

| | |
|---|---|
| *design firm* | John Champ Design Associates |
| *designer* | Randall Cohen |
| *art director* | John Champ |
| *client* | Hospital Associates |
| *logo for* | Corporate identity. |

112.4

| | |
|---|---|
| *design firm* | John Champ Design Associates |
| *designers* | Randall Cohen, Diana Kauzlarich |
| *art director* | John Champ |
| *client* | Corporate Meeting Concepts |
| *logo for* | Corporate identity. |

113.1

| | |
|---|---|
| *design firm* | John Champ Design Associates |
| *designer* | Randall Cohen |
| *client* | Hayer/Magnus Architects |
| *logo for* | Corporate identity. |

113.2

| | |
|---|---|
| *design firm* | MJR Associates |
| *designer* | Aimee McKirdy |
| *art director* | Frank Ruiz |
| *client* | Facility Designs |
| *logo for* | Corporate identity used on stationery, signage and marketing materials. |

113.3

| | |
|---|---|
| *design firm* | ComCorp, Inc. |
| *designer* | ComCorp Staff |
| *art director* | Debbie Werner |
| *client* | China Television Ventures |
| *logo for* | Corporate material. |

113.4

| | |
|---|---|
| *design firm* | Seaman Design Group |
| *designer* | Robin Seaman |
| *client* | Container.com |
| *logo for* | A national company involved in the rental and sales of portable steel storage containers. |

113.5

| | |
|---|---|
| *design firm* | Stephgrafx |
| *designer* | Stephanie Payan |
| *client* | Cheyenne Pools |
| *logo for* | Local swimming pool contract builder. |

113.1

FACILITY
DESIGNS

113.2

CHINA
TELEVISION
VENTURES

113.3

113.4

CHEYENNE POOLS
CRAFTSMANSHIP

113.5

JAHN INVESTMENT
ADVISORS

*114.1*

Good Vibes!
Promotions

*114.2*

HOT Z®

THERE'S MORE IN IT™

*114.3*

LAGUNA ART MUSEUM

*114.4*

115.1

ORANGE COUNTY

museum of art

115.2

BMJ

Baker, Manock & Jensen

ATTORNEYS AT LAW

115.3

*114.1*

| | |
|---|---|
| *design firm* | Benita Oberg Design |
| *designer* | Benita Oberg |
| *client* | Jahn Investment Advisors |
| *logo for* | Stationery, business cards, letterhead, envelopes, collateral (newsletters). |

*114.2*

| | |
|---|---|
| *design firm* | Deluxe Brand |
| *designer* | Tor Naerheim |
| *client* | Good Vibes |
| *logo for* | Los Angeles club promotion. |

*114.3*

| | |
|---|---|
| *design firm* | Miriello Grafico, Inc. |
| *designer* | Chris Keeney |
| *art director* | Ron Miriello |
| *logo for* | Hot Z. |

*114.4*

| | |
|---|---|
| *design firm* | Mike Salisbury Communications |
| *designer* | Mike Salisbury |
| *illustrator* | Brian Sisson |
| *client* | Laguna Art Museum |

*115.1*

| | |
|---|---|
| *design firm* | Sandy Gin Design |
| *designer* | Sandy Gin |
| *client* | Sandy Gin Design |
| *logo for* | A design studio. |

*115.2*

| | |
|---|---|
| *design firm* | Mike Salisbury Communications |
| *designer* | Mike Salisbury |
| *illustrator* | Bob Maile |
| *client* | Orange County Museum of Art |

*115.3*

| | |
|---|---|
| *design firm* | Shields Design |
| *designer* | Charles Shields |
| *client* | Baker, Manock & Jensen |
| *logo for* | Law firm. |

**Broudy Printing Inc.**

SEE THE POWER OF FINE PRINTING

*116.1*

**WRIGHT WILLIAMS & KELLY**

*116.2*

**LIST ENGINEERING COMPANY**

Mechanical Consultants

*116.3*

*116.4*

THE SOCIETY OF ILLUSTRATORS OF LOS ANGELES

SOLA

*116.5*

117.1

117.2

117.3

*116.1*
*design firm* Lamfers & Associates
*designer* Missy Nery
*art director* Debra Lamfers
*client* Broudy Printing, Inc.
*logo for* Company identity and applications. Broudy Printing is high-end web and sheet-fed printer.

*116.2*
*design firm* The Wecker Group
*designer* Robert Wecker
*client* Wright, Williams & Kelly
*logo for* Signage, packaging, stationery, collateral, forms.

*116.3*
*design firm* The Wecker Group
*designer* Robert Wecker
*client* List Engineering Company
*logo for* Signage, stationery, forms.

*116.4*
*design firm* Lamfers & Associates
*designer* Missy Nery
*art director* Debra Lamfers
*client* Lamfers & Associates
*logo for* Company identity—applied to all print and electronic media for design firm.

*116.5*
*design firm* Paul Rogers
*designer* Paul Rogers
*client* Society of Illustrators Los Angeles
*logo for* Organization of illustrators.

*117.1*
*design firm* Innovative Design and Advertising
*designers* Susan Nickey-Newton, Kim Crossett-Neumann
*client* Industrial Technology Management, Inc.
*logo for* Letterhead, business cards, envelopes, etc.

*117.2*
*design firm* Mortensen Design
*designer* Diana L. Kauzlarich
*art director* Gordon Mortensen
*client* Junglee Corporation
*logo for* High-tech company.

*117.3*
*design firm* Lawless Graphic Design
*designer* John P. Lawless
*client* Accu-Times, Inc.
*logo for* Time recorders and devices suppliers.

118.1
*design firm* McElveney & Palozzi Design Group, Inc.
*designer* Jon Westfall
*art directors* William McElveney, Steve Polozzi
*client* McElveney & Palozzi Design Group, Inc.
*logo for* Letterhead, business cards, envelopes, sell sheets.

118.2
*design firm* Warren Group
*designers* Katherine Staats, Laura Mische
*art director* Linda Warren
*client* Creative Wonder
*logo for* Stationery.

118.3
*design firm* GDS Studio
*designer* Gary Solomon
*client* Burke Williams
*logo for* Signage, robes, uniforms, retail gift items, spa floor, all promotional materials.

119.1
*design firm* Curry Design Associates
*designer* Jason Scheideman
*client* WTA
*logo for* Typographers association.

119.2
*design firm* Juddesign
*designers* Eric Watanabe, Amy Williams
*art director* Patti Judd
*client* Dakota Group
*logo for* Full service marketing/communications organization.

119.3
*design firm* Miriello Grafico, Inc.
*designer* Dennis Garcia
*client* Technically Correct

119.4
*design firm* Eve Vrla Design
*designer* Eve Vrla
*client* The Eastridge Companies
*logo for* Stationery, brochures and signage for real estate services.

118.1

118.2

118.3

W C A.

119.1

119.2

Technically

Correct

119.3

THE EASTRIDGE COMPANIES

119.4

120.1

120.2

120.3

120.1
*design firm* GDS Studio
*designer* Gary Solomon
*client* Net Advantage
*logo for* Interactive marketing solutions identity and promotion, website.

120.2
*design firm* Curry Design Associates
*designer* Pyong Mun
*client* Valuenet
*logo for* Online service software.

120.3
*design firm* Mortensen Design
*designer* Wendy Chon
*art director* Gordon Mortensen
*client* Growth Networks
*logo for* High-tech company.

121.1
*design firm* Engle + Murphy
*designer* Emily Moe
*client* Container.com
*logo for* Corporate ID for company that sells and leases oversized metal storage containers.

121.2
*design firm* Engle + Murphy
*designer* Robin Seaman
*client* Humana Worker's Compensation Services
*logo for* A division of Humana that assists in the process of returning injured workers to productive roles within the workplace.

121.3
*design firm* Engle + Murphy
*designer* Robin Seaman
*client* ebiocare.com
*logo for* E-commerce company that provides products and services to individuals with rare chronic disorders.

121.4
*design firm* Wolfback Design
*designer* Karin Scholz
*client* Waveband
*logo for* Corporate ID for a microwave optics corporation.

121.5
*design firm* McElveney & Palozzi Design Group, Inc.
*designer* Paul Reisinger, Jr.
*art directors* Steve Palozzi, Matt Nowicki
*client* LPA Software
*logo for* Brochure, tradeshow booth, website.

121.6
*design firm* Stone Yamashita
*designer* Jennifer Olsen
*art directors* Keith Yamashita, Robert Stone
*client* Hewlett-Packard
*logo for* E-speak, the technology embedded in devices to complete E-services.

121.1

121.2

121.3

121.4

121.5

121.6

OfficeClick.com[SM]

122.1

MarketSoft

122.2

pairgain
THE POWER BEHIND DSL ACCESS

122.3

cyberwerks
interactive

122.4

122.1
*design firm* Akagi Remington
*designer* Christopher Simmons
*art director* Doug Akagi
*client* OfficeClick.com
*logo for* Web portal for administrative assistants.

122.2
*design firm* Stewart Monderer Design, Inc.
*designer* Stewart Monderer
*client* MarketSoft Corporation
*logo for* Identity.

122.3
*design firm* Fuse
*designer* Mike Esparanza
*client* PairGain
*logo for* Corporate identity/brand, used in both print and digital mediums.

122.4
*design firm* Morreal Graphic Design
*designer* Mary Lou Morreal
*client* Cyberwerks Interactive
*logo for* Stationery, packaging, collateral.

123.1
*design firm* Shields Design
*designer* Charles Shields
*art director* Stephanie Wong
*client* Protosource Network
*logo for* Internet service provider.

123.2
*design firm* Shields Design
*designers* Thomas Kimmelman, Charles Shields
*art director* Stephanie Wong
*client* Digital Production Group
*logo for* Multimedia facilities.

123.3
*design firm* Zamboo
*designer* David Zambotti
*client* Direct Digital Communications
*logo for* Corporate identity.

123.4
*design firm* VWA Group
*designer* Rhonda Warren
*client* Connect.com
*logo for* High speed telecommunications access.

123.1

123.2

123.3

123.4

124.1
*design firm* Fitch
*designer* Cris Logan
*art director* Valloula Vasiliou
*client* Kärna LLC
*logo for* Corporate identity and product endorsement, stationery and web use for an innovative precision technology company.

124.2
*design firm* The Wecker Group
*designer* Robert Wecker
*client* Universal Internet
*logo for* Signage, stationery, form, collateral.

124.3
*design firm* Miriello Grafico, Inc.
*designer* Chris Keeney
*client* Microlink

125.1
*design firm* McElveney & Palozzi Design Group, Inc.
*art directors* William McElveney, Lisa Williamson
*client* PC Assistance, Inc.
*logo for* Letterhead, business cards, envelopes, brochure, containment folder.

125.2
*design firm* Morreal Graphic Design
*designer* Mary Lou Morreal
*client* SOMC Group Inc.
*logo for* Stationery, signage, collateral materials for Software of the Month Club.

125.3
*design firm* Stewart Monderer Design, Inc.
*designer* Aime Lecusay
*art director* Stewart Monderer
*client* eCredit.com, Inc.
*logo for* Identity.

124.1

124.2

124.3

PC Assistance
INCORPORATED

125.1

software of the month club®
somc
group inc.

125.2

e
Credit.com

125.3

126.1

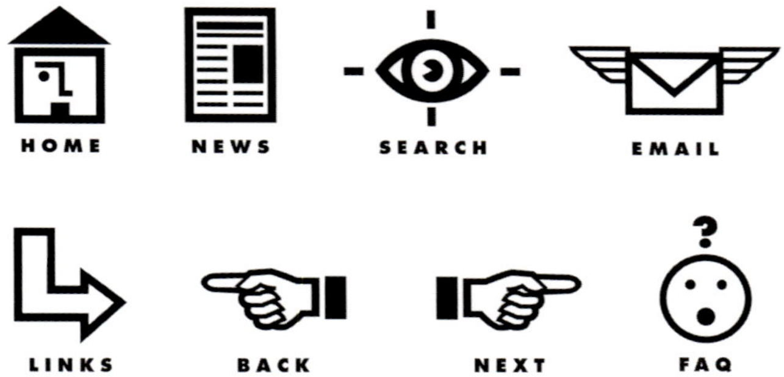


126.2

126.3

126.1
*design firm* Oh Boy, A Design Company
*designer* Alice Chang
*art director* David Salanitro
*client* Novo Interactive
*logo for* Business papers, website.

126.2
*design firm* Morreal Graphic Design
*designer* Mary Lou Morreal
*client* Bright Ideas
*logo for* Magazine & website.

126.3
*design firm* Morreal Graphic Design
*designer* Mary Lou Morreal
*client* Bright Ideas
*logo for* Magazine.

127.1
*design firm* Fitch
*designers* Cris Logan, Kian Kuan
*art director* Vassoula Vasiliou
*client* Be Incorporated
*logo for* Company and software identity system, packaging, marketing material, web. PC operating system icon.

127.2
*design firm* Alexander Atkins Design, Inc.
*designer* Alexander Atkins
*client* Capri Systems
*logo for* Systems integration company that develops advanced call centers.

127.3
*design firm* Stewart Monderer Design, Inc.
*designer* Stewart Monderer
*client* Electronic Book Technologies, Inc.
*logo for* Identity.

127.4
*design firm* LF Banks + Associates
*designer* John German
*art director* Lori F. Banks
*client* @Risk, Inc.
*logo for* Corporate identity for data mining company.

Be

*127.1*

capri systems

*127.2*

ebt

*127.3*

@RISK
SolutionsThroughDataMining

*127.4*

128.1

128.2

128.3

128.4

128.1

| | |
|---|---|
| *design firm* | LF Banks + Associates |
| *designer* | John German |
| *art director* | Lori F. Banks |
| *client* | BileniaTech, LP |
| *logo for* | Corporate identity for company that handles technology needs for businesses. |

128.2

| | |
|---|---|
| *design firm* | Fuse |
| *designer* | Russell Pierce |
| *client* | Fuse |
| *logo for* | Identity/brand for digital and print mediums. |

128.3

| | |
|---|---|
| *design firm* | Foreshock |
| *designer* | Gary Zdeneck |
| *client* | Foreshock |
| *logo for* | Company identity for print and web. |

128.4

| | |
|---|---|
| *design firm* | Lawless Graphic Design |
| *designer* | John P. Lawless |
| *client* | Lasertrek |
| *logo for* | Laser tag business. |

129.1

| | |
|---|---|
| *design firm* | Mike Salisbury Communications |
| *designer* | Tor Naerheim |
| *art director* | Mike Salisbury |
| *illustrator* | Derek Harven |
| *client* | Bungie |
| *logo for* | Halo computer game. |

129.2

| | |
|---|---|
| *design firm* | Earlywine Design |
| *designer* | Terry Earlywine |
| *client* | Warman Commercial Building Engineer |
| *logo for* | Company identity, stationery, signage. |

129.3

| | |
|---|---|
| *design firm* | The Illusion Factory |
| *designers* | Sahak Ekshian, Karen Ann Toal |
| *art director* | Brian Weiner |
| *illustrator* | Sahak Ekshian |
| *client* | The Illusion Factory |
| *logo for* | All corporate ID, brochure, bus card, letterhead, website, motion logo for video and film. |

129.4

| | |
|---|---|
| *design firm* | ComCorp, Inc. |
| *designer* | ComCorp Staff |
| *art director* | Abby Mines |
| *client* | MLP Network, Inc. |
| *logo for* | Corporate material. |

129.5

| | |
|---|---|
| *design firm* | Earlywine Design |
| *designer* | Terry Earlywine |
| *client* | International Sparc Technology Seminars |
| *logo for* | Tradeshow collateral, signage, stationery. |

*129.1*

*129.2*

*129.3*

*129.4*

*129.5*

130.1

130.2

130.3

130.4

130.5

MSP #618

*130.1*
*design firm* Talbot Design Group
*designer* Chris Kosman
*art director* GayLyn Talbot
*client* Traveler's Telecom
*logo for* New product—"Smart Suite." (product sheets, stationery, advertising, trade show collateral), website.

*130.2*
*design firm* Curry Design Associates
*designer* Jason Scheideman
*art director* Steve Curry
*client* Core Software
*logo for* Global imaging software.

*130.3*
*design firm* Tharp Did It
*designers* Rick Tharp, Debra Naeve
*client* NuTryx
*logo for* Internet training for senior citizens.

*130.4*
*design firm* Klass Design
*designer* Logo Doctor
*art director* Tim Clark
*illustrator* Teri Klass
*client* Crash Tech
*logo for* Identity for Mac repair technician.

*130.5*
*design firm* Michael Osborne Design
*designer* Andy Cambouris
*art director* Michael Osborne
*client* Enginewear, Inc.
*logo for* Women's sportswear.

*131.1*
*design firm* Boardwalk
*designer* Harriet Breitborde
*client* Channel Surfing
*logo for* Signage, on-air promotion marketing.

*131.2*
*design firm* Tharp Did It
*designers* Rick Tharp, Phillip Kim
*art director* Stephanie Paulson/The Stephenz Group
*client* Xerox
*logo for* Identifying a video conferencing technology.

*131.3*
*design firm* Curry Design Associates
*designer* Pyong Mun
*art director* Steve Curry
*client* Interactive Video Technologies
*logo for* Video broadcast on the Internet.

*131.1*

*131.2*

*131.3*

*132.1*
*design firm* B3 Design
*designer* Barbara B. Breashears
*client* Burton Valley Elementary P.T.A.
*logo for* Swingin' Into 2000 silent/live auction/fundraising.

*132.2*
*design firm* Seaman Design Group
*designer* Robin Seaman
*client* Voice Center for Arts and Medicine
*logo for* A medical facility that specializes in the treatment of singers and actors.

*132.3*
*design firm* Fuse
*designer* Kristi Kamei
*client* Yamaha Drums
*logo for* Overall corporate identity/brand used in both print and digital mediums.

*133.1*
*design firm* Innovative Design and Advertising
*designers* Susan Nickey-Newton, Kim Crossett-Neumannn
*client* ABC—5th Floor Production Music Library
*logo for* Corporate identity, business cards, stationery, CD labels, etc.

*133.2*
*design firm* Klass Design
*designer* Logo Doctor
*art directors* Tim Clark, Teri Klass
*illustrator* Tim Clark
*client* The Toledo Band
*logo for* Proposed identity and promotion for club band.

*133.3*
*design firm* Vigon/Ellis
*designer* Brian Jackson
*art director* Larry Vigon
*client* Welk Resort Center
*logo for* Corporate identity.

*133.4*
*design firm* Kevin Akers Designs
*designer* Kevin Akers
*client* San Francisco Symphony
*logo for* Chorus 25th Anniversary.

*132.1*

*132.2*

*132.3*

FIFTH FLOOR
PRODUCTION MUSIC LIBRARY

*133.1*

THE TOLEDO BAND

*133.2*

WELK RESORT CENTER

*133.3*

SAN FRANCISCO SYMPHONY
CHORUS
25th ANNIVERSARY

*133.4*

134.1

134.2

*134.1*
*design firm* Sabingrafik, Inc.
*designer* Dann Wilson
*illustrator* Tracy Sabin
*client* Jake's Jam
*logo for* A musical performance.

*134.2*
*design firm* The Wecker Group
*designer* Robert Wecker
*client* Cask One Vineyards
*logo for* Labels, packaging.

*135.1*
*design firm* Klass Design
*designer* Logo Doctor
*art director* Teri Klass
*illustrator* Tim Clark
*client* Karaoke Kim
*logo for* Identity for a bar.

*135.2*
*design firm* Seineger Design
*designer* Logo Doctor
*art director* Tony Seineger
*illustrator* Tim Clark
*client* Dreamgirls Production
*logo for* Poster.

*135.3*
*design firm* Vigon/Ellis
*designer* Marc Yeh
*art director* Larry Vigon
*client* Fleetwood Music
*logo for* Corporate identity.

*135.1*

*135.2*

*135.3*

136.1

136.2

136.3

| 136.1 | |
|---|---|
| *design firm* | Calori & Vanden-Eynden |
| *designers* | Chris Calori, David Vanden-Eynden |
| *client* | Gig Wear Store |
| *logo for* | Retailer of rock and roll memorabilia. |

| 136.2 | |
|---|---|
| *design firm* | Kevin Akers Designs |
| *designer* | Kevin Akers |
| *client* | San Francisco Symphony |
| *logo for* | Asian tour 1999. |

| 136.3 | |
|---|---|
| *design firm* | Kevin Akers Designs |
| *designer* | Kevin Akers |
| *client* | San Francisco Symphony |
| *logo for* | T-shirts promoting SFS-Greatful Dead members concert. |

| 137.1 | |
|---|---|
| *design firm* | Kevin Akers Designs |
| *designer* | Kevin Akers |
| *client* | San Francisco Symphony |
| *logo for* | Holiday program icon. |

| 137.2 | |
|---|---|
| *design firm* | Kevin Akers Designs |
| *designer* | Kevin Akers |
| *client* | San Francisco Symphony |
| *logo for* | European concert tour. |

137.1

137.2

*138.1*
*design firm* David Carter Graphic Design
*designer* Tien Pham
*art director* Lori Wilson
*client* Atlantis Resort and Casino
*logo for* Atlas Bar & Grill/Nassau, The Bahamas.

*138.2*
*design firm* Crouch & Naegli
*art directors* Jim Crouch, Jim Naegli
*illustrator* Tracy Sabin
*client* University of California at San Diego
*logo for* Tritons sports team.

*138.3*
*design firm* Focus Design
*designer* Brian Jacobson
*client* Appearance Salon
*logo for* Retail identity.

*139.1*
*design firm* Robert Miles Runyon
*designer* Logo Doctor
*art director* Tom Devine
*illustrator* Tim Clark
*client* Caesar's Palace
*logo for* Merchandising for Las Vegas hotel.

*139.2*
*design firm* David Carter Graphic Design
*designer* Tien Pham
*art director* Lori Wilson
*client* Disney Cruise Line
*logo for* Quarter Masters.

*139.3*
*design firm* VWA Group
*designer* Brian Blankenship
*art director* Rhonda Warren
*client* Quicksilver
*logo for* Identity, letterhead, automobile application, brochure.

*139.4*
*design firm* Michael Osborne Design
*designer* Andy Cambouris
*art director* Michael Osborne
*illustrator* Carolyn Vibbert
*client* Money Heaven
*logo for* Venture capital.

*138.1*

*138.2*

*138.3*

CAESARS PALACE

139.1

Quarter Masters

QUICKSILVER
MOBILE CAR WASH AND DETAIL

139.2

139.3

money heaven

139.4

140.1
*design firm* Kevin Akers Designs
*designer* Kevin Akers
*client* Tulips Express
*logo for* Air shipping/tulip bulbs company.

140.2
*design firm* Allen Orr
*designer* Allen Orr
*client* Valley Mailing Service

140.3
*design firm* Lorenz
*designer* Arne Ratermanis
*client* Gowan Seed Company
*logo for* Company identity.

141.1
*design firm* Stephgrafx
*designer* Stephanie Payan
*client* Palmer Group/Kathryn Fulhorst
*logo for* Landscape architect.

141.2
*design firm* Kevin Akers Designs
*designer* Kevin Akers
*client* Country Growers
*logo for* Nursery/hot house.

141.3
*design firm* The Wecker Group
*designer* Robert Wecker
*client* Canterbury Woods
*logo for* All applications.

141.4
*design firm* ComCorp, Inc.
*designer* Dave Lawrence
*art director* Debbie Werner
*client* FMC Corporation
*logo for* Corporate material.

140.1

140.2

140.3

141.1

141.2

CANTERBURY WOODS
A RETIREMENT RESIDENCE

141.3

PeaCommander

141.4

MONTEREY PENINSULA CHAMBER OF COMMERCE

142.1

monterey.com, Inc.
MONTEREY PENINSULA
ON-LINE GUIDE
monterey.com, Inc.

142.2

TRAILS

142.3

LANDSCAPE INNOVATIONS

142.4

AMBROSIA
taste life

142.5

The Forest Foundation

143.1

NEW LEAF PAPER

143.2

ALCALA

143.3

*142.1*
*design firm* The Wecker Group
*designer* Robert Wecker
*client* Monterey Peninsula Chamber of Commerce
*logo for* Stationery, signage, forms.

*142.2*
*design firm* The Wecker Group
*designer* Robert Wecker
*client* Monterey.com, Inc.
*logo for* Stationery, signage, collateral.

*142.3*
*design firm* Juddesign
*designer* Eric Watanabe
*art director* Patti Judd
*client* McMillin Company—Trails
*logo for* Residential real estate development.

*142.4*
*design firm* Alexander Atkins Design, Inc.
*designer* Alexander Atkins
*client* Landscape Innovations
*logo for* Landscaping design company.

*142.5*
*design firm* Tsuchiya Sloneker Communications, Inc.
*designer* Colin O'Neill
*art director* Julie Tsuchiya
*illustrator* Colin O'Neill
*client* Ambrosia
*logo for* Corporate identity—stationery system, ads, collateral, website.

*143.1*
*design firm* Pat Davis Design
*designer* Josh Glasgow
*client* California Forest Products
*logo for* Business systems.

*143.2*
*design firm* Elixir Design
*designer* Nathan Durrant
*art director* Jennifer Jerde
*illustrator* Nathan Durrant
*client* New Leaf Paper
*logo for* Company that manufactures and distributes high-quality environmentally responsible paper.

*143.3*
*design firm* Juddesign
*designer* Eric Watanabe
*art director* Patti Judd
*client* McMillin Company—Alcala
*logo for* Residential real estate development.

144.1

144.2

144.3

144.4

144.1

*design firm* The Wecker Group
*designer* Matt Gnibus
*art director* Rober Wecker
*client* Monterey Bay Kayaks
*logo for* T-shirts.

144.2

*design firm* Moonlight Design
*designer* David Ryer
*client* The Bone Marrow Foundation
*logo for* Non-profit organization offering support services to patients requiring bone marrow transplants, and their families.

144.3

*design firm* McElveney & Palozzi Design Group, Inc.
*designer* Jan Marie Gallagher
*art directors* William McElveney, Lisa Parenti
*client* LeRoy Village Green
*logo for* Letterhead, business cards, envelopes, pocket folder, brochure, tradeshow booth.

144.4

*design firm* Nita Ybarra Design
*designer* Nita Ybarra
*client* AnyIsland.com
*logo for* E-commerce, Internet, business.

MSP #545

145.1

*design firm* Seaman Design Group
*designer* Robin Seaman
*client* City of Orange Redevelopment Agency
*logo for* Agency that visually demonstrates movement, change and rebirth.

145.2

*design firm* MJR Associates
*designer* Frank Ruiz
*client* Cranberry Marketing Committee
*logo for* Corporate identity used on stationery and marketing materials.

145.3

*design firm* John Sposato Design & Illustration
*designer* John Sposato
*art director* Loretta Leiva
*illustrator* John Sposato
*client* John Wiley & Sons
*logo for* A line of financial advice products.

145.4

*design firm* Elixir Design
*designer* Nathan Durrant
*art director* Jennifer Jerde
*client* Grandiflorum Perfumes
*logo for* Perfumer specializing in custom-blended, all-natural fragrances.

145.1

CRANBERRY
MARKETING
COMMITTEE
UNITED STATES OF AMERICA

145.2

WILEY PERSONAL FINANCE SOLUTIONS

145.3

GRANDIFLORUM
PERFUMES

145.4

146.1

146.2

146.3

146.4

*146.1*
*design firm* Dutch Design
*designer* Rick Smits
*client* St. Margaret Mercy Hospital
*logo for* Proposed logo for fund-raising marathon T-shirt.

*146.2*
*design firm* Susan Meshberg Graphic Design
*designer* Susan Meshberg
*illustrator* Richard Mechanik
*client* 67 Wine & Spirits
*logo for* Retail liquor store.

*146.3*
*design firm* Dean Mitchell Design
*designer* Dean Mitchell
*illustrators* Steve Schadt, Alberto Zavallos
*client* PAR Broadcasting
*logo for* New Rock-format station.

*146.4*
*design firm* Wolfback Design
*designer* Karin Scholz
*client* Grace Hopper
*logo for* Conference celebrating women in computer science.

*147.1*
*design firm* David Carter Graphic Design
*designer* Sharon LeJeune
*art director* Lori Wilson
*client* Atlantis Resort and Casino
*logo for* 5 Twins/Nassau, The Bahamas.

*147.2*
*design firm* Michael Osborne Design
*designer* Michelle Regenbogen
*art director* Michael Osborne
*client* San Francisco Museum of Modern Art
*logo for* Merchandise 2000.

*147.3*
*design firm* The Wecker Group
*designer* Robert Wecker
*client* Meeting Professionals International
*logo for* Northern California Chapter/stationery, collateral.

*147.4*
*design firm* ComCorp, Inc.
*designer* Ron Alikpala
*art director* Abby Mines
*client* Chicago Manufacturing Center
*logo for* 1999 Year of the Small Manufacturer Conference (web, print, video).

147.2

147.1

147.3

147.4

148.1
*design firm* Zamboo
*designer* Becca Bootes
*art director* Dave Zambotti
*client* Premiere Dental Group
*logo for* Corporate identity.

148.2
*design firm* Kevin Akers Designs
*designer* Kevin Akers
*client* Inland Heart Center
*logo for* Cardiac care hospital.

148.3
*design firm* Zamboo
*designer* Becca Bootes
*art director* Dave Zambotti
*client* Tops Restaurant
*logo for* Corporate identity.

149.1
*design firm* Moonlight Design
*designer* David Ryer
*client* Futuredontics
*logo for* Portal website serving as search engine and directory for dentists and dental services (consumer and business-to-business).

149.2
*design firm* Allen Orr
*designer* Allen Orr
*client* SCS Dental Supply

149.3
*design firm* Sandy Gin Design
*designer* Sandy Gin
*client* Origin Medsystems
*logo for* Cardiovascular products at a medical device company.

149.4
*design firm* Stephgrafx
*designer* Stephanie Payan
*client* Southwest Medical Transcription
*logo for* Medical records transcription.

149.5
*design firm* BobCo Design Inc.
*designer* Robert S. Nenninger
*client* BobCo Design Inc.
*logo for* Corporate identity for a graphic design firm.

*148.1*

*148.2*

*148.3*

Dent-Net
THE INTERNET DENTAL RESOURCE

149.1

149.2

149.3

149.4

BobCo Design Inc

149.5

VerSecure

150.1

Ann E. James

MARKETING SERVICES

150.2

MAGIC HOUR

PICTURES

150.3

VISA MAGIC MOMENTS

150.4

ROSIE

150.5

151.1

151.2

151.3

*150.1*
*design firm* Mortensen Design
*designer* Diana L. Kauzlarich
*art director* Gordon Mortensen
*client* Hewlett-Packard (Versecure)
*logo for* High-tech company.

*150.2*
*design firm* Earlywine Design
*designer* Terry Earlywine
*client* Ann James Marketing Services
*logo for* Company identity, stationery.

*150.3*
*design firm* Warren Group
*designers* Jeanne Boyes, Laura Mische
*art director* Linda Warren
*client* Magic Hour Pictures
*logo for* Stationery, film intro.

*150.4*
*design firm* Frankel & Company
*designer* Logo Doctor
*art director* Diane Marshall
*illustrator* Tim Clark, Teri Klass
*client* Visa
*logo for* Incentive promotional campaign.

*150.5*
*design firm* Alexander Atkins Design, Inc.
*designer* Alexander Atkins
*client* Menlo College
*logo for* Library research service.

*151.1*
*design firm* Alexander Atkins Design, Inc.
*designer* Alexander Atkins
*client* Wind River Systems
*logo for* Software conference.

*151.2*
*design firm* Kevin Akers Designs
*designer* Kevin Akers
*client* Goddess Perfume Co.
*logo for* Monaco—women's cosmetics.

*151.3*
*design firm* Allen Orr
*designer* Allen Orr
*client* Cole Optometry
*logo for* Children's optometrist.

INSITES

INSITES

INSITES

INSITES

152.1

152.2

153.1

153.2

153.3

152.1

| | |
|---|---|
| *design firm* | Stone Yamashita |
| *designer* | Jennifer Olsen |
| *client* | Insites |
| *logo for* | Company that organizes all aspects of events, conferences, speech writing, etc. |

MSP #279

152.2

| | |
|---|---|
| *design firm* | Kevin Akers Designs |
| *designer* | Kevin Akers |
| *client* | Chevron |
| *logo for* | Maintenance manager for truck maintenance program. |

153.1

| | |
|---|---|
| *design firm* | The Wecker Group |
| *designer* | Robert Wecker |
| *client* | Monterey Peninsula School District |
| *logo for* | Stationery, forms. |

153.2

| | |
|---|---|
| *design firm* | Kevin Akers Designs |
| *designer* | Kevin Akers |
| *client* | Judee & Kevin's Wedding |
| *logo for* | Wedding invitation and related items. |

153.3

| | |
|---|---|
| *design firm* | Jeffry Hipp |
| *designer* | Jeffry Hipp |
| *client* | Backroad Antiques |
| *logo for* | Identity for an antiques store. |

154.1

154.2

154.3

154.4

154.1

| | |
|---|---|
| *design firm* | GDS Studio |
| *designer* | Gary Solomon |
| *client* | GSD Studio |
| *logo for* | Identity, stationery system and all promotion including website. |

154.2

| | |
|---|---|
| *design firm* | Boardwalk |
| *designer* | Harriet Breitborde |
| *client* | Pacific Park |
| *logo for* | Signage, marketing and advertising product applications for the theme park. |

154.3

| | |
|---|---|
| *design firm* | Moonlight Design |
| *designer* | David Ryer |
| *client* | Pension Resources |
| *logo for* | Company providing retirement fund management. |

154.4

| | |
|---|---|
| *design firm* | Sabingrafik, Inc. |
| *designer* | Tracy Sabin |
| *art director* | Marilee Bankert |
| *illustrator* | Tracy Sabin |
| *client* | Oliver McMillin |
| *logo for* | Retail/entertainment center. |

155.1

| | |
|---|---|
| *design firm* | Kevin Akers Designs |
| *designer* | Kevin Akers |
| *client* | San Francisco Symphony |
| *logo for* | Black & White Ball—charity event. |

155.1

THE MANSION
at MGM Grand

156.1

STAYWELL

156.2

SILVER PICTURES

156.3

1500 K STREET
THE SOUTHERN RAILWAY BUILDING

156.4

*156.1*
*design firm* David Carter Graphic Design
*designer* Ashley Barron
*art director* Lori Wilson
*client* The Mansion
*logo for* MGM Grand/Las Vegas, Nevada.

*156.2*
*design firm* Kevin Akers Designs
*designer* Kevin Akers
*client* StayWell
*logo for* Health publications company.

*156.3*
*design firm* Heart Times Coffee Cup Equals Lighting
*designer* Paul Rogers
*art director* Bobby Woods
*client* Silver Pictures
*logo for* Motion picture company.

*156.4*
*design firm* ComCorp, Inc.
*designer* ComCorp Staff
*art director* Abby Mines
*client* Jones Lang LaSalle
*logo for* Property marketing material.

*157.1*
*design firm* MJR Associates
*designer* Frank Ruiz
*client* Habanos Cigars
*logo for* Corporate identity used on stationery and marketing materials.

*157.2*
*design firm* Miriello Grafico, Inc.
*designer* Chris Keeney
*client* Spirit

*157.3*
*design firm* McElveney & Palozzi Design Group, Inc.
*art director* William McElveney, Lisa Parenti
*client* Abbott's Frozen Custard
*logo for* Posters, FSI's, coupons.

*157.4*
*design firm* MJR Associates
*designer* Frank Ruiz
*client* Hugs & Kisses
*logo for* Corporate identity used on stationery, signage and marketing materials.

HABANOS

the fine cigar people

157.1

SPIRIT

A Mind/Body Experience

a r u b a

157.2

GOTTA HAVE MY ABBOTT'S GOTTA HAVE MY ABBOTT'S

ABBOTT'S HABIT

157.3

Hugs & Kisses

COUNTRY GIFTS AND HOME DECOR

157.4

REGENTS COURT

158.1

ACCLAIM

158.2

FIRESTONE WALKER BREWING COMPANY

158.3

JEFFERSON AT Creekside

158.4

BELARIA

159.1

TECHNICOLOR.
THE GREATEST NAME IN COLOR

159.2

Touché &Co.

159.3

MIRABELLA

159.4

*158.1*
*design firm* VWA Group
*designer* Brian Blankenship
*art director* Rhonda Warren
*client* Lincoln Property Company
*logo for* Identity, letterhead, brochure for Regents Court.

*158.2*
*design firm* Moonlight Design
*designer* David Ryer
*client* International Interior Design Association
*logo for* Juried annual award given by interior designers to creators/manufacturers of new furniture, finishes and accessories.

*158.3*
*design firm* Pierre Rademaker Design
*designers* Pierre Rademaker, Marci Russo
*client* Firestone Walker Brewery
*logo for* Signage, print items, packaging.

*158.4*
*design firm* VWA Group
*designer* Brian Blankenship
*art director* Rhonda Warren
*client* Jefferson Property Inc.
*logo for* Identity, letterhead, brochure for Jefferson at Creekside.

MSP #608
*159.1*
*design firm* Susan Meshberg Graphic Design
*designer* Susan Meshberg
*client* Bel Canto Fancy Foods Ltd.
*logo for* Packaging product line of specialty food importer.

*159.2*
*design firm* Tsuchiya Sloneker Communications, Inc.
*designer* Matthew Schneider
*art directors* Mark Sloneker, Julie Tsuchiya
*illustrators* Matthew Schneider, Colin O'Neill
*client* Technicolor
*logo for* Corporate identity package, film, packaging.

*159.3*
*design firm* Bryan Friel Studio
*designer* Bryan Friel
*client* Touché
*logo for* Signage, garment tags, corporate literature.

*159.4*
*design firm* VWA Group
*designer* Rhonda Warren
*illustrator* Lem Lo
*client* JPI
*logo for* Luxury apartment homes.

THE KEN ROBERTS INSTITUTE

160.1

BANK OF PETALUMA

160.2

ENVIRONMENTAL PERSPECTIVES

160.3

The Smittcamp Family
HONORS COLLEGE
California State University, Fresno

160.4

| 160.1 | |
|---|---|
| *design firm* | Shields Design |
| *designer* | Charles Shields |
| *illustrator* | Doug Hansen |
| *client* | The Ken Roberts Company |
| *logo for* | Investment program. |

| 160.2 | |
|---|---|
| *design firm* | Mortensen Design |
| *designer* | Wendy Chon |
| *art director* | Gordon Mortensen |
| *client* | Bank of Petaluma |
| *logo for* | The bank. |

| 160.3 | |
|---|---|
| *design firm* | The Stricklin Companies |
| *designer* | Julie Ann Stricklin |
| *art director* | Ilsa House |
| *client* | Environmental Perspectives |
| *logo for* | Identity package. |

| 160.4 | |
|---|---|
| *design firm* | Shields Design |
| *designer* | Charles Shields |
| *art director* | Stephanie Wong |
| *illustrator* | Doug Hansen |
| *client* | Smittcamp Family Honors College |
| *logo for* | Honors College. |

| 161.1 | |
|---|---|
| *design firm* | Marv Cooper Design |
| *art director* | Doug Hardenburg |
| *illustrator* | Tracy Sabin |
| *logo for* | A restaurant featuring a wood-fired grill. |

| 161.2 | |
|---|---|
| *design firm* | Idea Place |
| *designer* | Paul Rogers |
| *art director* | Jon Sparmann |
| *illustrator* | Paul Rogers |
| *client* | Populuxe Productions |
| *logo for* | Film production company. |

| 161.3 | |
|---|---|
| *design firm* | Michael Osborne Design |
| *designer* | Michelle Regenbogen |
| *art director* | Michael Osborne |
| *illustrator* | Michelle Regenbogen |
| *client* | USS Hornet Museum |
| *logo for* | Museum store merchandise. |

| 161.4 | |
|---|---|
| *design firm* | Lorenz |
| *designer* | Arne Ratermanis |
| *client* | Janda & Garrington, LLC |
| *logo for* | Company identity. |

161.1

161.2

161.3

161.4

162.1

162.2

162.3

162.1

| | |
|---|---|
| *design firm* | Tyler Blik Design |
| *art directors* | Ron Fleming, Tyler Blik |
| *illustrator* | Tracy Sabin |
| *client* | Otay Ranch |
| *logo for* | Housing development. |

162.2

| | |
|---|---|
| *design firm* | Matthews/Mark |
| *designers* | Jon Meyers, Tracy Sabin |
| *illustrator* | Tracy Sabin |
| *client* | Eastlake Trails |
| *logo for* | A housing development. |

162.3

| | |
|---|---|
| *design firm* | Sabingrafik, Inc. |
| *designer* | Tracy Sabin |
| *art director* | Mirilee Bankert |
| *illustrator* | Tracy Sabin |
| *client* | Oliver McMillin |
| *logo for* | Shopping center. |

163.1

| | |
|---|---|
| *design firm* | The Wecker Group |
| *designer* | Robert Wecker |
| *illustrator* | Harry Briggs |
| *client* | Saucy Ree's Gourmet Foods |
| *logo for* | Packaging, stationery. |

163.2

| | |
|---|---|
| *design firm* | Shields Design |
| *designer* | Charles Shields |
| *art director* | Stephanie Wong |
| *illustrator* | Doug Hansen |
| *client* | Gold Coast Pistachios |
| *logo for* | Pistachio grower. |

163.3

| | |
|---|---|
| *design firm* | McElveney & Palozzi Design Group, Inc. |
| *art directors* | Steve Palozzi, Matt Nowicki |
| *client* | Genessee Brewing Company |
| *logo for* | Packaging—High Falls. |

*163.1*

*163.2*

*163.3*

164.1
*design firm* The Flowers Group
*designer* Cory Shehan
*illustrator* Tracy Sabin
*client* The Ridge
*logo for* Rustic golf resort.

164.2
*design firm* Conover
*designers* Carlos Avina, Amy Williams
*art director* David Conover
*illustrator* Dan Thoner
*client* Eldorado Stone
*logo for* Manufacturer of stone veneers.

164.3
*design firm* Pierre Rademaker Design
*art director* Pierre Rademaker
*client* Solvang Visitors & Convention Bureau
*logo for* Print items, souvenirs, outdoor boards, collateral.

165.1
*design firm* Pierre Rademaker Design
*designers* Pierre Rademaker, Debbie Shibata
*client* San Luis Obispo Chamber of Commerce
*logo for* Promotional gift items, souvenirs, apparel.

165.2
*design firm* Pierre Rademaker Design
*designers* Pierre Rademaker, Jeff Austin
*client* Paso Robles Inn
*logo for* Print items, advertising, signage, outdoor boards.

165.3
*design firm* Pierre Rademaker Design
*designers* Pierre Rademaker, Jeff Austin
*client* Ocean View Flowers
*logo for* Print items, product tags, packaging, advertising, vehicles, signage.

165.4
*design firm* Shields Design
*designer* Charles Shields
*illustrator* Doug Hansen
*client* Great Pacific Trading Company
*logo for* Investments company.

*164.1*

*164.2*

*164.3*

165.1

165.2

165.3

165.4

CARLSBAD BY THE SEA
Retirement Community

166.1

CANNERY ROW INN

166.2

CYPRESS TREE INN

166.3

166.1

| | |
|---|---|
| *design firm* | Juddesign |
| *art director* | Patti Judd |
| *client* | Carlsbad By The Sea |
| *logo for* | Retirement community. |

166.2

| | |
|---|---|
| *design firm* | The Wecker Group |
| *designer* | Robert Wecker |
| *illustrator* | Mark Savee |
| *client* | Cannery Row Inn |
| *logo for* | Signage, stationery. |

166.3

| | |
|---|---|
| *design firm* | The Wecker Group |
| *designer* | Robert Wecker |
| *client* | Cypress Tree Inn |
| *logo for* | Signage, stationery. |

167.1

| | |
|---|---|
| *design firm* | Vitro/Robertson |
| *art director* | Jeff Payne |
| *illustrator* | Tracy Sabin |
| *client* | Rubio's Baja Grill |
| *logo for* | Matchbook cover for a TV spot. |

167.2

| | |
|---|---|
| *design firm* | GDS Studio |
| *designer* | Gary Solomon |
| *art director* | Jerry Cowart |
| *illustrator* | Gary Solomon |
| *client* | Candle Corporation |
| *logo for* | Annual sweepstakes trip vacation, this time to Aruba. |

167.3

| | |
|---|---|
| *design firm* | Sabingrafik, Inc. |
| *designer* | Tracy Sabin |
| *art director* | Marilee Bankert |
| *illustrator* | Tracy Sabin |
| *client* | Oliver McMillin |
| *logo for* | Shopping center/entertainment complex. |

167.1

167.2

167.3

*168.1*

| | |
|---|---|
| *design firm* | The Alfstad Blank Group |
| *designer* | Logo Doctor |
| *art director* | Chuck Moore |
| *illustrators* | Tim Clark, Teri Klass |
| *client* | MantaRay |
| *logo for* | Software packaging. |

*168.2*

| | |
|---|---|
| *design firm* | Tharp Did It |
| *designers* | Rick Tharp, Nicole Coleman |
| *client* | Steamer's The Grillhouse |
| *logo for* | Restaurant signage, menus, apparel. |

*168.3*

| | |
|---|---|
| *design firm* | Klass Design |
| *designer* | Logo Doctor |
| *art director* | Teri Klass |
| *illustrators* | Tim Clark, Teri Klass |
| *client* | Splash Entertainment |
| *logo for* | Identity for a production company. |

*169.1*

| | |
|---|---|
| *design firm* | David Carter Graphic Design |
| *designer* | Tien Pham |
| *art director* | Lori Wilson |
| *client* | Atlantis Resort and Casino |
| *logo for* | Fathoms/Nassau, The Bahamas. |

*169.2*

| | |
|---|---|
| *design firm* | BobCo Design Inc. |
| *designer* | Robert S. Nenninger |
| *client* | Fishking, Inc. |
| *logo for* | Corporate identity for a Japanese-owned fish processing company in Los Angeles. |

*169.3*

| | |
|---|---|
| *design firm* | The Wecker Group |
| *designers* | Robert Wecker, Matt Gnibus |
| *client* | Aquafuture, Inc. |
| *logo for* | All applications. |

*169.4*

| | |
|---|---|
| *design firm* | The Wecker Group |
| *designers* | Robert Wecker, Matt Gnibus |
| *client* | Aquafuture, Inc. |
| *logo for* | All applications. |

*168.1*

*168.2*

*168.3*

FATHOMS

169.1

Fishking

AQUAFUTURE™

169.2

169.3

AQUARESEARCH

169.4

Isla Nena

170.1

CowboySushi

170.2

SEACASTLE
SANTA MONICA

170.3

bluefin
CAFE & BILLIARDS

170.4

*170.1*
*design firm* VWA Group
*designer* Rhonda Warren
*client* Isla Mena
*logo for* Pool grill at luxury resort.

*170.2*
*design firm* Blanco Design
*designer* Shelly Blanco
*client* Cowboy Sushi Restaurant

*170.3*
*design firm* Vigon/Ellis
*designer* Marc Yeh
*art director* Larry Vigon
*client* SeaCastle
*logo for* Corporate identity.

*170.4*
*design firm* The Wecker Group
*designer* Robert Wecker
*client* Blue Fin Billiards
*logo for* All applications.

*171.1*
*design firm* De Muth Design
*designer* Roger De Muth
*art director* Betsy Borba
*illustrator* Roger De Muth
*client* Articulations/RCC Foods
*logo for* Seamore Fish identity image.

*171.2*
*design firm* Dean Mitchell Design
*designer* Dean Mitchell
*illustrator* Jon W. Wright
*client* Daiwa Fishing Tackle
*logo for* 1999 Catalog.

*171.3*
*design firm* The Wecker Group
*designer* Robert Wecker
*client* Blue Fin Billiards
*logo for* Signage, T-shirts.

*171.1*

*171.2*

*171.3*

*172.1*
*design firm* Akagi Remington
*designer* Dorothy Remington
*client* Tides Foundation
*logo for* New identity for the Tides Foundation and Tides Center, partners with donors to increase and organize resources for social change.

*172.2*
*design firm* Wolfback Design
*designer* Karin Scholz
*client* VM Labs
*logo for* Corporate ID for company in 3D-rendering technology for video games.

*172.3*
*design firm* Kevin Akers Designs
*designer* Kevin Akers
*client* Armanino McKenna
*logo for* CPA firm.

*173.1*
*design firm* The Wecker Group
*designer* Robert Wecker
*client* Monterey Pacific, Inc.
*logo for* Signage, stationery, forms.

*173.2*
*design firm* Alexander Atkins Design, Inc.
*designer* Alexander Atkins
*client* Alexander Atkins Design, Inc.
*logo for* Graphic design studio.

*173.3*
*design firm* Eve Vrla Design
*designer* Eve Vrla
*client* Mitsui Components (USA), Inc.
*logo for* Corporate identity, signage and packaging for automotive recycling plant.

*173.4*
*design firm* MJR Associates
*designer* Frank Ruiz
*client* Ponderosa Telephone
*logo for* Corporate identity used on stationery, signage and marketing materials.

TIDES
FOUNDATION

*172.1*

VM LABS

*172.2*

ARMANINO MCKENNA LLP
Certified Public Accountants & Consultants

*172.3*

MONTEREY PACIFIC
APPLIED
AGRICULTURAL
TECHNOLOGIES

173.1

173.2

MITSUI
Components (U.S.A.), Inc.

173.3

Ponderosa Telephone

173.4

Bidcom

CENTRAL VALLEY BUSINESS INCUBATOR INCORPORATED

GROWING NEW VENTURES

174.1

174.2

DARIN IVERSON, DDS, LTD

174.3

SFMOMA

©SFMOMA 1996

SAN FRANCISCO MUSEUM OF MODERN ART

174.4

175.1

175.2

175.3

174.1

| | |
|---|---|
| *design firm* | Michael Osborne Design |
| *designer* | Andy Cambouris |
| *art director* | Michael Osborne |
| *client* | Bidcom |
| *logo for* | E-commerce. |

174.2

| | |
|---|---|
| *design firm* | Shields Design |
| *designer* | Charles Shields |
| *art director* | Stephanie Wong |
| *client* | Central Valley Business Incubator |
| *logo for* | Entrepreneurial facilities. |

174.3

| | |
|---|---|
| *design firm* | Innovative Design and Advertising |
| *designers* | Mimi, Susan Nickey-Newton |
| *art director* | Kim Crossett-Neumann |
| *client* | Darin Iverson, DDS, LTD |
| *logo for* | All corporate identity needs for orthodontist. |

174.4

| | |
|---|---|
| *design firm* | Michael Osborne Design |
| *designer* | Michael Osborne |
| *client* | San Francisco Museum of Modern Art |
| *logo for* | Museum store. |

175.1

| | |
|---|---|
| *design firm* | Juddesign |
| *designer* | Vicki Wyatt |
| *art director* | Patti Judd |
| *client* | Sun 'n' Sand |
| *logo for* | Volleyball sportswear/team uniforms. |

175..2

| | |
|---|---|
| *design firm* | Kevin Akers Designs |
| *designer* | Kevin Akers |
| *client* | Lombard Brokerage |
| *logo for* | Online brokerage company. |

175.3

| | |
|---|---|
| *design firm* | Mortensen Design |
| *designer* | Wendy Chon |
| *art director* | Gordon Mortensen |
| *client* | Kit Cole Investment Advisory Services |
| *logo for* | Financial investment services. |

176.1

176.2

176.3

176.4

*176.1*
*design firm* Fuse
*designer* Russell Pierce
*client* Centricity
*logo for* Overall corporate identity/brand, used in both print and digital mediums.

*176.2*
*design firm* Engle + Murphy
*designer* Emily Moe
*client* Centricomp
*logo for* Corporate ID for workers' compensation insurance company.

*176.3*
*design firm* Dutch Design
*designer* Rick Smits
*client* JW Builders
*logo for* Business cards.

*176.4*
*design firm* Shimokochi/Reeves
*designer* Mamoru Shimokochi
*client* Zig Ziglar Network Trademark
*logo for* Zinera: branding identity & packaging system/nutritional supplements.

*177.1*
*design firm* Eve Vrla Design
*designer* Eve Vrla
*client* Victoria Crawford
*logo for* Stationery and brochures for personal counseling business.

*177.2*
*design firm* Talbot Design Group
*designer* Chris Kosman
*art director* GayLyn Talbot
*client* Biometric Identification
*logo for* Identity and collateral.

*177.3*
*design firm* Shields Design
*designer* Charles Shields
*art director* Stephanie Wong
*client* Heberger & Company, Inc.
*logo for* Accounting firm.

*177.4*
*design firm* Stephgrafx
*designer* Stephanie Payan
*client* M Marketing Inc./Biokeys
*logo for* Pharmaceutical company.

*177.5*
*design firm* J. Robert Faulkner Advertising
*designer* J. Robert Faulkner
*client* Spellbound

the way of discovery

177.1

bioMETRIC
identification

177.2

HEBERGER
& COMPANY
Certified Public Accountants

177.3

BIOKEYS
PHARMACEUTICALS

177.4

Strategic Event Design Spellbound Public Relations Marketing

177.5

178.1

178.2

178.3

178.4

178.5

178.1
*design firm* Stone Yamashita
*designer* Jennifer Olsen
*client* Tickmark Solutions
*logo for* Business cards, letterheads, all print and web media for accounting services company.

178.2
*design firm* Tsuchiya Sloneker Communications, Inc.
*designer* Andrew Harding
*art director* Julie Tsuchiya
*illustrators* Andrew Harding, Julie Tsuchiya
*client* Ecast, Inc.
*logo for* Product identity—ads, website, collateral.

178.3
*design firm* Tsuchiya Sloneker Communications, Inc.
*designer* Doug Ridgway
*art director* Mark Sloneker
*illustrator* Doug Ridgway
*client* Evocative, Inc.
*logo for* Corporate identity, stationery system, collateral, website.

178.4
*design firm* Vigon/Ellis
*designer* Marc Yeh
*art director* Larry Vigon
*client* Pronounced Technologies Inc.
*logo for* Corporate identity.

178.5
*design firm* Conover
*designer* Carlos Avina
*art director* David Conover
*client* Sejerson DPS
*logo for* Digital film processor.

179.1
*design firm* Design Firm Alexander Atkins Design, Inc.
*designer* Alexander Atkins
*client* Stanford University
*logo for* Organization providing activities, services and benefits to alumni.

179.2
*design firm* Vigon/Ellis
*designer* Brian Jackson
*art director* Larry Vigon
*client* DIVA Systems Inc.
*logo for* Corporate identity.

179.3
*design firm* Taber Integrative Design
*designer* Michele Taber
*client* California Fair Services Authority
*logo for* Proposed logo for an organization providing members with specialized support services.

*179.1*

*179.2*

*179.3*

*180.1*
*design firm* B3 Design
*designer* Barbara B. Breashears
*client* Dolce Mia
*logo for* Handmade frames & collectibles.

*180.2*
*design firm* Bruce Yelaska Design
*designer* Bruce Yelaska
*client* Hunan Garden
*logo for* Chinese restaurant.

*180.3*
*design firm* The Wecker Group
*designer* Robert Wecker
*client* Ryan Ranch Rotisserie
*logo for* Signage, menus, stationery.

*181.1*
*design firm* McElveney & Palozzi Design Group, Inc.
*art directors* Steve Palozzi, Lisa Parenti
*client* Genessee Brewing Company
*logo for* Packaging and P.O.P. materials, sell sheets—Genny Summer Brew.

*181.2*
*design firm* McElveney & Palozzi Design Group, Inc.
*art directors* Steve Palozzi, Matt Garrity
*client* Genessee Brewing Company
*logo for* Packaging and P.O.P. materials, sell sheets—Genny Winter Brew.

*181.3*
*design firm* Pierre Rademaker Design
*designers* Pierre Rademaker, Marci Russo
*client* Mrs. Weinstein's Toffee
*logo for* Print items, product packaging, advertising.

*181.4*
*design firm* Dutch Design
*designer* Rick Smits
*client* Terpstra Custom Kitchens
*logo for* Stationery, business cards and vehicle graphics.

*181.5*
*design firm* Lawless Graphic Design
*designer* John P. Lawless
*client* Albany-Colonie Regional Chamber of Commerce
*logo for* Promotion and celebration of the 100th anniversary in the year 2000 of the Albany-Colonie chapter of the Chamber of Commerce.

*181.6*
*design firm* Mike Salisbury Communications
*designer* Mike Salisbury
*client* Jurassic Park

*180.1*

*180.2*

*180.3*

181.1

181.2

181.3

181.4

181.5

181.6

Western Bagel
SINCE 1947

182.1

McHale Design

182.2

PASSPORT
TO SUCCESS

182.3

SNEAKY PETE'S

182.4

EXCLUSIVE MANUFACTURER FOR MASTERPIECE COOKIES
Internationally
DELICIOUS, INC.

182.5

GREAT
EXPECTATIONS
LIGHTING Co.

182.6

*182.1*
*design firm* GDS Studio
*designer* Gary Solomon
*client* Western Bagel
*logo for* Signage, uniforms, cups, mugs, trucks.

*182.2*
*design firm* Blanco Design
*designer* Shelly Blanco
*client* McHale Design

*182.3*
*design firm* Earlywine Design
*designer* Terry Earlywine
*client* SCO (Santa Cruz Operation)
*logo for* Product resellers program, packaging and collateral.

182.4
*00.0*
*design firm* Lawless Graphic Design
*designer* John P. Lawless
*client* Sneaky Pete's
*logo for* Popular area nightclub in Albany, New York.

*182.5*
*design firm* B3 Design
*designer* Barbara B. Breashears
*client* Internationally Delicious, Inc.
*logo for* Stationery, etc. for cookie manufacturer of Masterpiece Cookies.

*182.6*
*design firm* The Wecker Group
*designer* Robert Wecker
*client* Great Expectations Lighting Co.
*logo for* Stationery.

*183.1*
*design firm* J. Robert Faulkner Advertising
*designer* J. Robert Faulkner
*illustrator* Alex Marshall
*client* Scriveners' Society

*183.2*
*design firm* Boardwalk
*designer* Harriet Breitborde
*client* Staples Center
*logo for* Marketing/promotion and signage.

*183.3*
*design firm* Sabingrafik, Inc.
*designer* Tracy Sabin
*art director* Van Oliver
*illustrator* Tracy Sabin
*client* Uptown CarWash
*logo for* A carwash company.

*183.1*

*183.2*

*183.3*

design firm | The Stricklin Companies
designers | Ann Stricklin, Tom Allen
art director | Steve Emtman
client | American Family Film Foundation
logo for | Charity identity for promotion, web site, marketing packages.

184.2
design firm | Lorenz
designer | Arne Ratermanis
client | Monarch Brewery, LLC
logo for | Restaurant identity.

184.3
design firm | The Wecker Group
designers | Robert Wecker, Matt Gnibus
client | The DoubleTree Hotel/Monterey
logo for | Pub signage, menus, specialty advertising.

185.1
design firm | Mires Design
art director | José Serrano
illustrator | Tracy Sabin
client | Troop 260, Boy Scouts of America
logo for | T-shirt.

185.2
design firm | Shields Design
designer | Charles Shields
illustrator | Doug Hansen
client | Trinidad Cigar Emporio
logo for | Cigar company.

185.3
design firm | Maddochs & Co.
art director | Clare Sebenius
illustrator | Tracy Sabin
client | El Cholo
logo for | Mexican cantina.

185.4
design firm | The Wecker Group
designer | Robert Wecker
client | The Hearth Shop
logo for | Signage, stationery.

185.5
design firm | David Carter Graphic Design
client | Paris Resort and Casino
logo for | La Rotisserie Des Artistes/Las Vegas, Nevada.

184.1

184.2

184.3

185.1

185.2

185.3

185.4

185.5

WALL STREET
MAIN STREET
MAIN STREET
TRADING COMPANY

186.1

RUNNING IRON
RESTAURANT AND SALOON

186.2

Watt Farms
COUNTRY MARKET

186.3

186.1

| | |
|---|---|
| *design firm* | Shields Design |
| *designer* | Charles Shields |
| *illustrator* | David Wariner |
| *client* | Main Street Trading Company |
| *logo for* | Investment company. |

186.2

| | |
|---|---|
| *design firm* | The Wecker Group |
| *designer* | Robert Wecker |
| *illustrator* | Mark Savee |
| *client* | Running Iron Restaurant |
| *logo for* | Signage, T-shirts. |

186.3

| | |
|---|---|
| *design firm* | McElveney & Palozzi Design Group, Inc. |
| *art directors* | William McElveney, Jon Westfall |
| *client* | Watt Farms Country Market |
| *logo for* | Letterhead, business cards, envelopes. |

187.1

| | |
|---|---|
| *design firm* | Primo Angeli Inc. |
| *designers* | Kelson Mau, Philippe Becker |
| *art director* | Rich Scheve |
| *client* | Ben & Jerry's |
| *logo for* | Ben & Jerry's ice cream cartons. |

187.2

| | |
|---|---|
| *design firm* | Primo Angeli Inc. |
| *designers* | Koji Miyaki, Harumi Kubo |
| *art director* | Steve Lindsay |
| *client* | Pharmavite |
| *logo for* | Nature Made. |

187.3

| | |
|---|---|
| *design firm* | Primo Angeli Inc. |
| *designers* | Jasmine Gerber, Toby Sudduth |
| *art director* | Steve Lindsay |
| *client* | PowerBar Inc. |
| *logo for* | Perform. |

*187.1*

*187.2*

*187.3*

*188.1*
*design firm* The Wecker Group
*designer* Robert Wecker
*illustrator* Mark Savee
*client* Red's Donuts
*logo for* Signage, packaging, forms.

*188.2*
*design firm* Leeson Design
*designer* Susan Leeson
*client* Franklin's Family Auto Care
*logo for* Family-owned auto repair shop.

*188.3*
*design firm* The Wecker Group
*designer* Robert Wecker
*client* Caruso's Corner
*logo for* All applications.

*189.1*
*design firm* Jeffry Hipp
*designer* Jeffry Hipp
*client* Model T Ford Club of American
*logo for* Inland Empire Chapter/Flivvers 'n Rivers, the MTFCA's Western National tour. Logo and embroidered patch.

*189.2*
*design firm* Shields Design
*designer* Charles Shields
*client* The Ken Roberts Company
*logo for* Investment program.

*189.3*
*design firm* Lawless Graphic Design
*designer* John P. Lawless
*client* Seacrets
*logo for* Popular under 21 night club.

*189.4*
*design firm* McElveney & Palozzi Design Group, Inc.
*art directors* William McElveney, Ellen Johnson
*client* Fieldbrook Farms, Inc.
*logo for* Sell sheets.

*188.1*

*188.2*

*188.3*

*189.1*

*89.2*

*189.3*

*189.4*

190.1

190.2

190.3

190.1

| | |
|---|---|
| *design firm* | Wolfback Design |
| *designer* | Karin Scholz |
| *client* | Institute for Women & Technology |
| *logo for* | Corporate ID for organization promoting growth and revolutionary ideas in technology. |

190.2

| | |
|---|---|
| *design firm* | Bruce Yelaska Design |
| *designer* | Bruce Yelaska |
| *client* | Bikram's Yoga College of India |
| *logo for* | Yoga school. |

190.3

| | |
|---|---|
| *design firm* | Tsuchiya Sloneker Communications, Inc. |
| *designer* | Andrew Harding |
| *art director* | Julie Tsuchiya |
| *illustrator* | Andrew Harding |
| *client* | Ecast, Inc. |
| *logo for* | Corporate identity—stationery system, collateral, website, ads. |

191.1

| | |
|---|---|
| *design firm* | Alexander Atkins, Inc. |
| *designer* | Alexander Atkins |
| *client* | Spiral Communications |
| *logo for* | Public relations firm. |

191.2

| | |
|---|---|
| *design firm* | Tom Fowler, Inc. |
| *designer* | Elizabeth P. Ball |
| *client* | IBC |
| *logo for* | Conveying the emerging interactive relationship between Unilever HPC's consumers, customers and suppliers. |

SPIRAL
COMMUNICATIONS

191.1

ibc
Interactive Brand Center

191.2

*192.1*
*design firm* Morreal Graphic Design
*designer* Mary Lou Morreal
*client* Upper Deck
*logo for* Trading card.

*192.2*
*design firm* Kevin Akers Designs
*designer* Kevin Akers
*client* Jack Lemmon Invitational Golf Tournament
*logo for* Celebrity golf tournament in Pebble Beach, California.

*192.3*
*design firm* Disney Consumer Products
*designer* Logo Doctor
*art director* Kirsti Ronback
*illustrator* Teri Klass
*client* Los Angeles Angels
*logo for* Merchandising.

*193.1*
*design firm* The Wecker Group
*designer* Robert Wecker
*client* Carmel Valley Inn & Tennis Resort

*193.2*
*design firm* The Wecker Group
*designer* Robert Wecker
*client* Pacific Grove Rotary Club
*logo for* Event signage.

*193.3*
*design firm* Shields Design
*designer* Charles Shields
*client* The Zone Sportsplex
*logo for* Sports facility.

*193.4*
*design firm* Allen Orr
*designer* Allen Orr
*client* Olympic Soccer 2000 Australia
*logo for* Student project.

*193.5*
*design firm* The Wecker Group
*designer* Robert Wecker
*client* City of Monterey
*logo for* Signage, stationery, forms.

*192.1*

*192.2*

*192.3*

CARMEL VALLEY INN & TENNIS RESORT

193.1

SUNSET TENNIS CLASSIC

193.2

THE ZONE™
SPORTSPLEX

193.3

193.4

MONTEREY SPORTS CENTER

193.5

HONDA
GRAND PRIX OF MONTEREY
FEATURING THE Shell 300

194.1

ALLCAR
MOTORSPORTS
BOBBY ALLISON / DAVE CARROLL MOTORSPORTS

194.2

HONDA
GRAND PRIX OF MONTEREY
FEATURING THE TEXACO / HAVOLINE 300

194.3

C·A·R·T ®

194.4

MALIBU GRAND PRIX

194.5

195.1

195.2

195.3

*194.1*
*design firm* The Wecker Group
*designer* Robert Wecker
*client* Laguna Seca Raceway
*logo for* Signage, programs, TV advertising.

*194.2*
*design firm* The Wecker Group
*designer* Robert Wecker
*client* Allcar Motor Sports
*logo for* All applications.

*194.3*
*design firm* The Wecker Group
*designer* Robert Wecker
*client* Laguna Seca Raceway
*logo for* Signage, programs, TV advertising.

*194.4*
*design firm* Primo Angeli Inc.
*designer* Philippe Becker
*art director* Carlo Pagoda
*client* Championship Auto Racing Team Inc.
*logo for* Championship auto racing team.

*194.5*
*design firm* Mike Salisbury Communications
*designer* Logo Doctor
*art director* Mike Salisbury
*illustrator* Tim Clark
*client* Malibu Grand Prix
*logo for* Promotional event.

*195.1*
*design firm* Studio Seireeni
*designer* Logo Doctor
*art director* Rick Seireeni
*illustrator* Tim Clark
*client* NY Knicks
*logo for* Proposed identity for merchandising.

*195.2*
*design firm* Pierre Rademaker Design
*designers* Pierre Rademaker, Jeff Austin
*client* USA Sports Mecca
*logo for* Print items, apparel, collateral.

*195.3*
*design firm* Mires Design
*art directors* John Ball, Myles McGuinness
*illustrator* Tracy Sabin
*client* Harcourt Brace & Co.
*logo for* Children's literature book.

NANCY**LOPEZ**GOLF™

196.1

PALMER | GOLF

BUILT TO HIT IT

196.2

196.3

*196.1*

| | |
|---|---|
| *design firm* | Miriello Grafico, Inc. |
| *designer* | Courtney Mayer |
| *art director* | Ron Miriello |
| *client* | Nancy Lopez Golf |
| *logo for* | Various marketing materials, exhibit materials and product identity. |

*196.2*

| | |
|---|---|
| *design firm* | Miriello Grafico, Inc. |
| *designers* | Courtney Mayer, Chris Keeney |
| *art director* | Ron Miriello |
| *client* | Arnold Palmer Golf |

*196.3*

| | |
|---|---|
| *design firm* | Kevin Akers Designs |
| *designer* | Kevin Akers |
| *client* | Mervyns California |
| *logo for* | Icon for men's clothing line. |

*197.1*

| | |
|---|---|
| *design firm* | GDS Studio |
| *designer* | Gary Solomon |
| *illustrator* | Chip Pace |
| *client* | Mono Lake Committee |
| *logo for* | Posters, racing jerseys, brochures to promote annual race on bicycles from LA to Mono Lake. |

*197.2*

| | |
|---|---|
| *design firm* | Vitro/Robertson |
| *art director* | John Bade |
| *illustrator* | Tracy Sabin |
| *client* | Shimano Resort |
| *logo for* | Promotion of summer activities at a family resort. |

*197.3*

| | |
|---|---|
| *design firm* | Bryan Friel Studio |
| *designer* | Bryan Friel |
| *client* | Washington State University Track & Field |
| *logo for* | Sportswear, posters. |

*197.1*

*197.2*

*197.3*

*198.1*

| | |
|---|---|
| *design firm* | Seaman Design Group |
| *designer* | Robin Seaman |
| *art director* | Dan Simon |
| *illustrator* | Robin Seaman |
| *client* | Los Angeles Dodgers |
| *logo for* | A new line of retail children's apparel called Dodgers Baby Blue. |

*198.2*

| | |
|---|---|
| *design firm* | Kevin Akers Designs |
| *designer* | Kevin Akers |
| *client* | Cross Training |
| *logo for* | Focus on the family magazine article on keeping teens fit. |

*198.3*

| | |
|---|---|
| *design firm* | Seaman Design Group |
| *designer* | Robin Seaman |
| *art director* | Dan Simon |
| *illustrator* | Robin Seaman |
| *client* | Los Angeles Dodgers |
| *logo for* | A new line of retail children's apparel called Dodgers Baby Blue. |

*199.1*

| | |
|---|---|
| *design firm* | Miriello Grafico, Inc. |
| *designer* | Dennis Garcia, Maximo Escobedo |
| *client* | San Diego Crew Classic |

*199.2*

| | |
|---|---|
| *design firm* | Jon Briggs Design |
| *designer* | Jon Briggs |
| *client* | The Upper Deck Company |
| *logo for* | Proposed logo for apparel line (T-shirts). |

*199.3*

| | |
|---|---|
| *design firm* | Kevin Akers Designs |
| *designer* | Kevin Akers |
| *client* | Motorcycle Industry Council |
| *logo for* | Promotion of motorcycle sports. |

*198.1*

*198.2*

*198.3*

SAN DIEGO
CREW CLASSIC

199.1

takin' it to the
GLASS
1998-99 U.D. ATHLETIC

199.2

DISCOVER TODAY'S MOTORCYCLING

199.3

*200.1*
*design firm* John Champ Design Associates
*designer* Randall Cohen
*art director* Denise St. Louis
*illustrator* Randall Cohen
*client* KCBS/KLLC Radio Alice@97.3
*logo for* Event identity for festival and concert.

*200.2*
*design firm* Primo Angeli Inc.
*designer* Terrence Tong
*art director* Rich Scheve
*illustrator* Mark Jones
*client* Silicon Gaming
*logo for* Odyssey.

*200.3*
*design firm* Tsuchiya Sloneker Communications, Inc.
*designer* Dolin O'Neill
*art directors* Julie Tsuchiya, Mark Sloneker
*illustrator* Colin O'Neill
*client* Eastman Kodak/Themed Entertainment
*logo for* Service logo—collateral, film, trailers, ads.

*200.4*
*design firm* Kevin Akers Designs
*designer* Kevin Akers
*client* Gren Fed
*logo for* Offshore bank located in Grenada.

*201.1*
*design firm* Zamboo
*designers* Dave Zambotti, Chris Go
*art director* Becca Bootes
*client* SolSource Innovations
*logo for* Corporate identity.

*201.2*
*design firm* Stewart Monderer Design, Inc.
*designer* Aime Lecusay
*art director* Stewart Monderer
*client* League School of Greater Boston
*logo for* Identity.

*201.3*
*design firm* Fuse
*designer* Russell Pierce
*client* PairGain (Star Gazer)
*logo for* Software, used in digital mediums and packaging.

*201.4*
*design firm* Engle + Murphy
*designer* Emily Moe
*client* Pacific Western National Bank
*logo for* Corporate ID. The bank decided to update their logo and look for their 20th anniversary and new headquarters.

*200.1*

*200.2*

*200.3*

*200.4*

sōlsource®
INNOVATIONS

201.1

OF GREATER BOSTON
LEAGUE SCHOOL

201.2

StarGazer

201.3

PACIFIC WESTERN
*National Bank*

201.4

DANIEL LANE

Enrolled Agent
Financial and
Tax Planning

*"Your Road To Financial Success"*

202.1

CENTRAL CALIFORNIA
MERCY FLIGHT

202.2

DAVID
LOOP
EUROPEAN
PARTS & SERVICE

202.3

*202.1*
*design firm* The Wecker Group
*designer* Robert Wecker
*client* Daniel Lane
*logo for* Signage, stationery.

*202.2*
*design firm* The Wecker Group
*designer* Robert Wecker
*client* Mercy Flight/Central California
*logo for* Signage, stationery.

*202.3*
*design firm* The Wecker Group
*designer* Matt Gnibus
*art director* Robert Weckerc
*client* David Loop European
*logo for* Signage, stationery.

*203.1*
*design firm* Earlywine Design
*designer* Terry Earlywine
*client* Teknekron
*logo for* Client seminar "Strategic Direction."

*203.2*
*design firm* B3 Design
*designer* Barbara B. Breashears
*client* TR@KS
*logo for* Stationery system, computer kiosks, web design, etc. for Transportation Resources @ Kiosk Sites.

*203.3*
*design firm* Pierre Rademaker Design
*designers* Pierre Rademaker, Jeff Austin
*client* Sphere Gift Shop
*logo for* Print items, packaging, signage.

203.1

203.2

203.3

204.1

204.2

204.3

205.1

205.2

205.3

204.1
*design firm* Alexander Atkins Design, Inc.
*designer* Alexander Atkins
*client* College
*logo for* Orientation week at college.

204.2
*design firm* Seaman Design Group/Willardson & Assoc.
*designer* Robin Seaman
*art director* Dan Simon
*illustrator* Robin Seaman
*client* Limited Too
*logo for* Apparel signature identification designed for embroidery onto new line of camp shirts, graphics to have the same look and feel as for their adult apparel.

204.3
*design firm* Bryan Friel Studio
*designer* Bryan Friel
*client* Blue Yonder Tours
*logo for* Stationery, ads, promotional items.

205.1
*design firm* Kevin Akers Designs
*designer* Kevin Akers
*client* Passport Wine Club
*logo for* Wine-of-the-month-club.

205.2
*design firm* Discovery Design Group
*designer* Logo Doctor
*art director* Dan Cavey
*illustrators* Tim Clark, Teri Klass
*client* The Discovery Channel
*logo for* Press kit and on-air broadcast.

205.3
*design firm* Moonlight Design
*designer* Karen Ryan
*art director* David Ryer
*client* Barnstorm Entertainment
*logo for* Cross-media production company, including music, film and video.

206.1

206.2

206.3

*206.1*
*design firm* Curtis & Company
*designer* Logo Doctor
*art director* Joe Curtis
*illustrator* Teri Klass
*client* World Caravan Concepts
*logo for* Proposed identity.

*206.2*
*design firm* Kevin Akers Designs
*designer* Kevin Akers
*client* Santa Maria Shipping
*logo for* Shipping company,

*206.3*
*design firm* Sabingrafik, Inc.
*art director* Lisa Peters
*illustrator* Tracy Sabin
*client* Harcourt Brace & Co.
*logo for* Publisher's imprint.

*207.1*
*design firm* Pierre Rademaker Design
*designers* Pierre Rademaker, Jeff Austin
*client* Rusack Vineyards
*logo for* Wine labels, tasting room signage, point of purchase signage.

207.1

*208.1*
*design firm* Stoyan Design
*designer* Michael Stinson
*art director* David Wooters
*illustrator* Michael Stinson
*client* Virtrue

*208.2*
*design firm* McElveney & Palozzi Design Group, Inc.
*art directors* Steve Palozzi, Matt Nowicki
*client* Factura
*logo for* Sell sheets.

*208.3*
*design firm* Michael Osborne Design
*designer* Michelle Regenbogen
*art director* Michael Osborne
*client* Asera
*logo for* E-commerce.

*208.4*
*design firm* Michael Osborne Design
*designer* Nicole Lembi
*art director* Michael Osborne
*client* Vitessa
*logo for* E-commerce.

*209.1*
*design firm* Stewart Monderer Design, Inc.
*designer* Aime Lecusay
*art director* Stewart Monderer
*client* Expand Networks, Inc.
*logo for* Identity.

*209.2*
*design firm* Solution 111 Design
*designer* Darryl Glass
*client* Solution 111 Design
*logo for* Stationery for Solution 111 Design, a graphic design studio.

*209.3*
*design firm* Eve Vrla Design
*designer* Eve Vrla
*client* Ensemble
*logo for* Corporate identity for real estate firm.

*209.4*
*design firm* Juddesign
*designer* Eric Watanabe
*art director* Patti Judd
*client* Furniture Resources
*logo for* Commercial office furniture.

Virtrue

*208.1*

Alliance
BY FACTURA

*208.2*

AserA

*208.3*

vitessa

*208.4*

EXPAND
networks

209.1

SOLUTION 111
DESIGN

209.2

ENSEMBLE™
INVESTMENTS, LLC

209.3

furnituresources
BUSINESS FURNITURE SOLUTIONS

209.4

210.1

210.2

210.3

210.4

210.5

210.6

211.1

211.2

211.3

*10.1*
*design firm* Moonlight Design
*designer* Karen Ryan
*art director* David Ryer
*client* Keigre Studios
*logo for* A photographer.

*210.2*
*design firm* Sandy Gin Design
*designer* Sandy Gin
*client* bingwear
*logo for* A clothing company.

*210.3*
*design firm* Q Studio
*designer* Lan Khiew
*client* Okiwa Pro-Sound Version
*logo for* New corporate identity & products.

*210.4*
*design firm* Allen Orr
*designer* Allen Orr
*client* The Tara Theater
*logo for* The 40th anniversary of the movie Psycho.

*210.5*
*design firm* Deluxe Brand
*designer* Tor Naerheim
*client* Pimp Wear
*logo for* Line of clothing.

*210.6*
*design firm* Deluxe Brand
*designer* Tor Naerheim
*client* Deluxe Brand
*logo for* In-house Deluxe Brand identity.

*211.1*
*design firm* Fitch
*designer* Cris Logan
*art director* Vassoula Vasiliou
*client* Kärna LLC
*logo for* Product packaging, marketing materials, websites. Product icon for new gamer mouse-razer boomslang.

*211.2*
*design firm* Lorenz
*designer* Arne Ratermanis
*client* San Diego Christian Unified School District
*logo for* Fund raising event.

*211.3*
*design firm* Mortensen Design
*designer* Wendy Chon
*art director* Gordon Mortensen
*client* CallTheShots
*logo for* Internet company.

Deluxe

MARQUE DÉPOSÉE

212.1

212.2

ED WOOD

212.3

212.1

| | |
|---|---|
| *design firm* | Deluxe Brand |
| *designer* | Tor Naerheim |
| *client* | Deluxe Brand |
| *logo for* | In-house Deluxe Brand identity. |

212.2

| | |
|---|---|
| *design firm* | Elixir Design |
| *designer* | Jennifer Jerde |
| *illustrator* | Skylar Nielsen |
| *client* | Christian Dauer |
| *logo for* | Architect specializing in custom interiors and furniture. |

212.3

| | |
|---|---|
| *design firm* | Mike Salisbury Communications |
| *designer* | Mike Salisbury |
| *illustrator* | Brian Sisson |
| *client* | Disney |
| *logo for* | Ed Wood |

213.1

| | |
|---|---|
| *design firm* | Evolution Design |
| *art directors* | Bear Files, Annie Files |
| *client* | Garden Fresh Restaurant Corporation |
| *logo for* | Ladles Soup & Salad Takery—a new restaurant chain. |

213.2

| | |
|---|---|
| *design firm* | MJR Associates |
| *designer* | Frank Ruiz |
| *client* | Bayshore International |
| *logo for* | Corporate identity used on stationery, signage, vehicles, and marketing materials. |

213.3

| | |
|---|---|
| *design firm* | LF Banks + Associates |
| *designer* | Cesar Varela |
| *art director* | Lori F. Banks |
| *client* | LF Banks + Associates |
| *logo for* | Corporate identity for graphic design firm. |

213.4

| | |
|---|---|
| *design firm* | Primo Angeli Inc. |
| *designers* | Harumi Kubo, Toby Sudduth |
| *art director* | Steve Lindsay |
| *client* | PowerBar Inc. |
| *logo for* | Essentials. |

213.1

213.2

213.3

213.4

ONE RAFFLES LINK

214.1

GB

GUTTMAN & BLAEVOET
*Mechanical Engineers*

214.2

MAGIC LIVE!

214.3

KOKO KANU

214.4

JONELLE WEAVER

214.5

FIRSTEPS
MEDIATION CENTERS
ALTERNATIVES BY COMMUNICATING

215.1

ATHLETA

215.2

Z.CAVARICCI

215.3

*214.1*
*design firm* Calori & Vanden-Eynden
*designer* Chris Calori, Judy Gee
*art director* David Vanden-Eyden
*client* HongKong Land Limited
*logo for* Office building which encompasses both modern and classic architectural styles.

*214.2*
*design firm* Benita Oberg Design
*designer* Benita Oberg
*client* Guttman & Blaevoet
*logo for* Stationery, business cards, letterhead, envelopes, collateral, signage for mechanical engineers.

*214.3*
*design firm* Lawless Graphic Design
*designer* John P. Lawless
*client* Planet Magic Productions
*logo for* Magic Live, a series of magic shows at Historic Schenectady Theater (Proctors) featuring top national acts such as the Pendragons.

*214.4*
*design firm* Susan Meshberg Graphic Design
*designer* Susan Meshberg
*client* Carriage House Imports Ltd.
*logo for* Packaging (label) and promotion for a high-proof Rum.

*214.5*
*design firm* Elixir Design
*designer* Jennifer Tolo
*art director* Jennifer Jerde
*client* Jonelle Weaver Photography
*logo for* The photographer's still life work and her personal taste for old, out-of-the ordinary objects.

*215.1*
*design firm* Lawless Graphic Design
*designer* John P. Lawless
*client* First Steps Mediation Centers
*logo for* Mediation consultant firm for divorcing couples.

*215.2*
*design firm* Elixir Design
*designer* Nathan Durrant
*art director* Jennifer Jerde
*client* Athleta
*logo for* Women's sporting goods catalog.

*215.3*
*design firm* Inhouse Design Department
*designer* Lesli Wuco-B
*client* Z. Cavaricci Clothing
*logo for* Corporate/packaging & clothing labels/Website.

Fine Furnishings and Design
CLASSIC INTERIORS

216.1

THE
KEN ROBERTS
Gallery

216.2

*216.1*
*design firm* Conover
*designer* Amy Williams
*art director* David Conover
*client* Classic Interiors
*logo for* Interior design firm.

*216.2*
*design firm* Shields Design
*designer* Charles Shields
*client* The Ken Roberts Company
*logo for* Gallery.

*217.1*
*design firm* The Wecker Group
*designer* Robert Wecker
*client* The DoubleTree Hotel/Monterey
*logo for* Restaurant signage, menus.

*217.2*
*design firm* Stark Designs
*designer* Amy Stark
*client* Lena Fallica
*logo for* A house cleaning business.

*217.3*
*design firm* Pierre Rademaker Design
*designer* Pierre Rademaker, Jeff Austin
*client* Santa Barbara Farms
*logo for* Print items, advertising, shipping cartons, vehicles, product tags.

*217.4*
*design firm* Susan Meshberg Graphic Design
*designer* Susan Meshberg
*illustrator* Jia Hwang, Marie Hiraga
*client* Wedgie Dietetic Foods
*logo for* Product packaging for organic food line.

The California Grill

*217.1*

LENA'S CUSTOM CLEANING

*217.2*

SANTA BARBARA FARMS ™

*217.3*

Marty's ORGANIC

*217.4*

218.1

218.2

218.3

218.4

218.1
*design firm* Allen Orr
*designer* Allen Orr
*client* Tim Adkins Photography

218.2
*design firm* Calori & Vanden-Eynden
*designer* Gina De Benedittis
*art director* David Vanden-Eynden
*client* Inventure Place
*logo for* National Inventors Hall of Fame. Museum and hall of fame complex dedicated to discovery and invention.

218.3
*design firm* ComCorp, Inc.
*designer* Dave Lawrence
*art director* Debbie Werner
*client* Jones Lang LaSalle
*logo for* Property marketing material.

218.4
*design firm* Stoyan Design
*designer* Michael Stinson
*illustrator* Michael Stinson
*client* Stellar Road

219.1
*design firm* Bryan Friel Studio
*designer* Bryan Friel
*client* On The Mark Communications
*logo for* Marketing.

219.2
*design firm* Pat Davis Design
*designer* Susan Leeson
*client* Belle Cooledge Library
*logo for* Public library.

On the Mark
COMMUNICATIONS

219.1

Belle
Cooledge
LIBRARY

219.2

220.1

220.2

220.3

220.4

220.5

221.1

221.2

221.3

*220.1*
*design firm* Moonlight Design
*designer* David Ryer
*client* Rebel Planet Studios
*logo for* British film production company.

*220.2*
*design firm* The Marketing Store
*designer* Susan Leeson
*client* The Marketing Store
*logo for* Marketing/communications firm.

*220.3*
*design firm* Tharp Did It
*designers* Rick Tharp, Nicole Coleman
*client* divio
*logo for* Identifying video compression technology.

*220.4*
*design firm* Lawless Graphic Design
*designer* John P. Lawless
*client* Blue Mule Bar & Grill
*logo for* Business logo for bar and grill.

*220.5*
*design firm* Calori & Vanden-Eynden
*designer* Chris Calori, Denise Funaro
*client* Dark Horse Theater Company
*logo for* Small, regional theater company.

*221.1*
*design firm* Tom Fowler, Inc.
*designers* Thomas G. Fowler, Elizabeth P. Ball
*client* Haute Decor.com
*logo for* Company that facilitates on-line sales of high quality home and office furnishings through virtual showrooms created by acclaimed interior designers.

*221.2*
*design firm* Lawless Graphic Design
*designer* John P. Lawless
*client* Mitchell Management Associates
*logo for* Marketing research firm.

*221.3*
*design firm* Calori & Vanden-Eynden
*designers* Chris Calori, David Vanden-Eyden
*client* PIG X Annual Pig Roast
*logo for* 10th annual pig roast and social event.

222.1

| | |
|---|---|
| *design firm* | The Wecker Group |
| *designer* | Robert Wecker |
| *client* | Soquel Creek Water District |
| *logo for* | Signage, stationery, forms. |

222.2

| | |
|---|---|
| *design firm* | The Wecker Group |
| *designer* | Robert Wecker |
| *client* | Carmel Area Waste Management District |
| *logo for* | All applications. |

222.3

| | |
|---|---|
| *design firm* | Vigon/Ellis |
| *designer* | Brian Jackson |
| *art director* | Larry Vigon |
| *client* | Pacific Coast Hotels |
| *logo for* | Corporate identity. |

223.1

| | |
|---|---|
| *design firm* | The Wecker Group |
| *designer* | Robert Wecker |
| *client* | Carmel Marina Corporation |
| *logo for* | All applications. |

223.2

| | |
|---|---|
| *design firm* | The Wecker Group |
| *designer* | Robert Wecker |
| *client* | Monterey Peninsula Water Management |
| *logo for* | Signage, stationery, collateral. |

223.3

| | |
|---|---|
| *design firm* | Innovative Design and Advertising |
| *designers* | Brandon Bennett, Susan Nickey-Newton |
| *art director* | Kim Crossett-Neumann |
| *client* | VICO |
| *logo for* | Labels and ads for pump (whirlpool) manufacturer to identify strength of their product. |

223.4

| | |
|---|---|
| *design firm* | The Wecker Group |
| *designer* | Robert Wecker |
| *client* | CSU Monterey Bay |
| *logo for* | Stationery. |

223.5

| | |
|---|---|
| *design firm* | Kevin Akers Designs |
| *designer* | Kevin Akers |
| *client* | Bay One Technologies |
| *logo for* | San Francisco-based software developer. |

*222.1*

*222.2*

*222.3*

CARMEL MARINA
CORPORATION

223.1

MONTEREY
PENINSULA
WATER
MANAGEMENT
DISTRICT

223.2

WOW!

whirlpool operating wonder

223.3

FRIENDS OF
CALIFORNIA STATE
UNIVERSITY
MONTEREY BAY

223.4

bay one technologies

223.5

224.1

224.2

224.3

224.4

224.1

| | |
|---|---|
| *design firm* | Tom Fowler, Inc. |
| *designer* | Karl S. Maruyama |
| *client* | Eventra |
| *logo for* | Differentiating Eventra from other commerce/electronic data interface companies and positioning it as a 21st century global EC/EOI player. |

224.2

| | |
|---|---|
| *design firm* | Focus Design |
| *designer* | Brian Jacobson |
| *client* | Annuncio Software |
| *logo for* | Corporate identity. |

224.3

| | |
|---|---|
| *design firm* | Allen Orr |
| *designer* | Allen Orr |
| *client* | Pondfish Fishstore |

224.4

| | |
|---|---|
| *design firm* | Sabingrafik, Inc. |
| *art director* | Lisa Peters |
| *illustrator* | Tracy Sabin |
| *client* | Harcourt Brace & Co. |
| *logo for* | Publisher's imprint. |